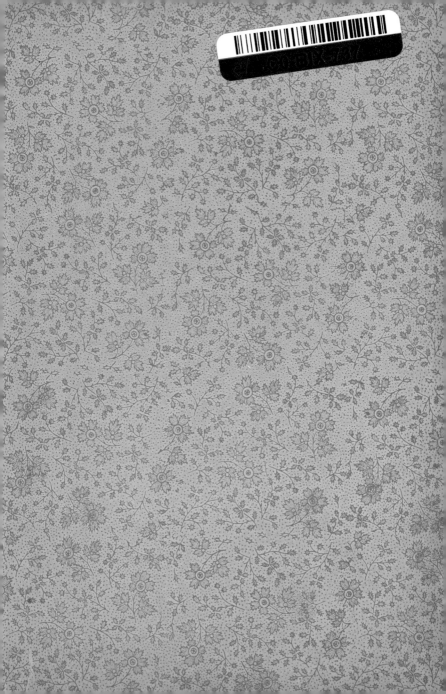

For my part I have no fear of the man.—Page 54

LITTLE PLAYS for LITTLE PLAYERS

EDITED BY

MATILDA BLAIR

NEW YORK
McLOUGHLIN BROTHERS

CONTENTS

1. Stage Properties are those articles which are used in a play either for scenery or for dress. One child should be appointed to look after these properties. He must see that they are in their proper places before the curtain rises and at hand as the scene goes on.

2. Each child is responsible for his own personal properties, that is to say, the articles of dress, swords, armour, etc., belonging to his part.

3. In setting or arranging the scenery, the Right is on the right hand and the Left on the left hand as you stand facing the stage, with your back to the audience.

4. The Prompter should stand out of sight of the audience, at the side of the stage, book in hand, ready to give the missing word or sentence, should any one forget his part.

Crowning the Queen

CROWNING THE QUEEN.

F. H. S.

'Tis dear merry May-time,
'Tis dear merry May-time,
  Our hearts are so happy to-day,
For bright sunny hours,
The scent of the flowers
  Give color and perfume to May!
We wait for our May Queen,
Our beautiful May Queen;
  We come here to crown her to-day,
Sweet blossoms we're bringing,
While gayly we're singing,
  To welcome our Queen of the May.
(The Queen approaches.)

  Chorus

Ah! here comes our May Queen,
Our beautiful May Queen!
  Rejoice, for she cometh this way,
With flowers well-laden,
O fair youth and maiden,
  Give welcome to Queen of the May!

7

Note—The children—arranged as partners—form two long lines along the path, through which the Queen is to approach the throne. (A pile of cushions, covered over with a piece of green cambric, surmounted by a layer of evergreen, may be made to serve the purpose very well.)

Over the throne, a child's hoop, twined with leaves and blossoms, and with cords—flower-trimmed—stretched across, like the diameters of a circle, may be suspended by ribbons from a hook in the ceiling, or it may be tacked firmly, by means of little braces as supports, to the upper ledge of a blackboard. Cords—flower-trimmed—extending from the circumference to the floor, and tacked firmly to it, will serve to steady the hoop, and add very materially to the canopy effect.

During the singing of the second stanza, two small boys step forward and place a crown of flowers upon the queen's head. This crown—which should hang in readiness over the arm of one of the boys—may be woven of green raffia, to give the correct shape—the front coming up in rather a blunt point, and tapering gradually towards the sides—daisies and buttercups—natural or artificial—grasses, and leaves may be intertwined to give a pleasing effect and completely hide the foundation. If natural flowers cannot be obtained, a very realistic effect may be had

with artificial daisies and buttercups, such as are
commonly placed on children's hats, or very sat-
isfactory ones may be made from colored tissue
paper.
(Girls curtsey, boys pay deep obeisance—hand
on heart.)

O welcome our May Queen,
Our beautiful May Queen,
　O crown her with blossoms so gay!
All　nature　is　singing,
Our　voices　are　ringing,
　In songs for this gladsome May day.

Come, wish for our May Queen,
Our　beautiful　May　Queen
　That life hold the joy of the May,
The　music,　the　flowers,
The　bright　sunny　hours,
　Shall gladden each year like the May.
(Place crown upon the Queen's head.)
Come, crown then our May Queen,
Our　beautiful　May　Queen,
　O crown her with blossoms to-day.
The garlands we're wreathing,
Their　faint　perfume　breathing
　Encircle our Queen of the May!

The children may provide themselves with garlands of natural flowers—or they may very easily make effective ones from colored tissue paper circles, folded into petals and twisted together with the fine wires that the florists use.

During the singing of the *chorus* in the *first* stanza, the Queen may enter from the rear of the room and pass between the two lines of waiting children.

Wooden hoops, such as come for embroidery frames—or those from small (five pound) butter boxes, twined with colored tissue papers, cambric, or silkolene, with cords stretched across, as in the large hoop for the Queen's canopy, may be used very effectively, if held uplifted by the children to form an arch under which the Queen shall pass to her throne.

SUGGESTION—During the singing of the second stanza, two small children should step forward to place the crown of flowers upon the Queen's head while the others move nearer and surround the throne on either side.

Come honor our May Queen,
Our beautiful May Queen!
    With flowers our homage now pay,
While gay hues are blending
The bright sunbeams lending
    A rainbow of color to-day.

Come wish for our May Queen,
Our beautiful May Queen,
    Since life cannot always be May—
That Hope ever glowing,
Like rainbow tints showing,
    May brighten the hours each day.

Chorus

(Repeat the chorus of the second stanza.)

Exit Queen, surrounded by the children, who follow skipping, and singing the melody to the syllables, "Tra-la-la," etc.

The Trooping of the Flowers

THE TROOPING OF THE FLOWERS.

F. H. S.

All.

We are coming, we are coming,
  Hear our little patt'ring feet,
Hosts of flowers, sweet and dainty,
  Coming bright May-time to greet.

First row (skip through the right hand aisle to the rear of the room, down through their own aisle, to former position, singing.)

NOTE—During the singing of the preceding stanza, the children imitate, with a light tripping movement (moving forward in the aisles.)—the "patt'ring feet" of the flowers.

We are violets, we are violets,
  Each in white, or purple hood,
See us droop our little faces
  As all modest violets should.

NOTE—Hoods fashioned of white or of purple tissue paper will add to the effect. If the heads are held a little inclined, or drooping, the words will mean more to the children as they sing them. Second row (follow in the same order as the preceding row, to former position, singing.)

We are cowslips, we are cowslips,
　　Dressed in brightest green and gold,
Cowslip's just a mimic name;
　　Our true name's March Marigold.

NOTE—Yellow caps and green ruffles of tissue paper will add to the effect. Third row (skip around to former position, singing.)

We are bluets, we are bluets,
　　"Quaker Ladies," quiet, shy;
"Innocents," some people call us,
　　As our baby eyes they spy.

Fourth row (skip around to former position, singing)

We are lilies, we are lilies,
　　See our little silvery bells
Ringing forth sweet fairy music
　　Of the woodland and the dells.

NOTE—The wild lily-of-the-valley—or the cultivated variety—may be the flower represented.
Have the children carry tiny bells which they chime in rythm with the melody. White tissue paper caps will add to the effect.

Fifth row (skip around to former position, singing.)

Dandelions, dandelions,
　　Come to show our yellow hair;
By and by the playful breezes
　　Will our little heads leave bare.

Note—Little fringed caps of yellow tissue paper will add to the effect.

Sixth row (skip around to former position, singing.)

Shy arbutus, shy arbutus,
  Pink and white with perfume sweet;
From our home 'neath leaves and mosses,
  We the gladsome sunlight greet.

Note—Caps made of pink and white tissue paper will add to the effect. Seventh row (skip around to former position, singing.)

Buttercups yellow, buttercups yellow,
  Bright as gold without, within,
We a message tell to children,
  When they hold us 'neath the chin.

Note—Bright yellow caps of tissue paper will add to the effect. Eighth row (skip around to former position, singing)

We are daisies, we are daisies,
  Each in little ruffled cap,
When the sun is high in heaven,
  Then we're glad to take a nap.

Note—Caps with yellow crowns and white pleated ruffles will add to the effect. (All stand in position in the aisles, while singing)

We are blossoms, we are blossoms,
  From the wood, the field, the glade,
Praise the Giver, praise the Father,
  Who these gifts in love hath made.

Humpty Dumpty

HUMPTY DUMPTY.

M. B.

This stage-play is for twelve boys from four to eight years of age. They are dressed in over-alls padded as full as possible about the waist, hips and legs. These "roly poly" boys wear little round straw hats with blue ribbons hanging off the brims, and have ruffs about the neck and ruffled blouses also padded about the body and arms.

A wall extends across the stage about two-thirds the distance from the footlights. The frame-work for this is made by setting large packing-boxes about three or four feet in height and uniform size along in a row with the bottoms towards the front of the stage, Across these boxes is tacked red building paper having the mortar for the "brick wall" marked off with white crayon or paint. If the former is used, dip the stick of crayon in water and use it wet, which will make the lines show off much better than if used dry. Hay or grass is strewn thickly about on the floor at the foot of the wall, and a tree or two may be placed back of it or near the ends,

by mounting each tree on a standard. Chairs
are placed back of the wall for the boys' use in
climbing upon the wall.

Pianist strikes a chord, and curtain rises, showing only this stage-setting.

Loud whispers are heard behind the wall and
the boys mount from the rear. They appear one
after another, climbing up so as to lie on top of
the box with one leg thrown over the wall and
hanging down in front, the other stretched along
the top of the wall. When all are in position
they leap up and stand in a line. The largest
boy is at one end and the smallest at the other.
Pianist plays any pretty march, and boys lift hats
and bow low in greeting to audience. After several bows they sit down on the wall with feet
hanging over in front.

The boys repeat each change throughout a musical period.

1. Boys clap right hands up and down on
knee in time to music, while looking gleefully
over their shoulders.

2. Boys cross legs, sit on their hands, and
rock back and forth in time to music, looking
down at floor in front of wall.

3. Boys sit on hands and crack heels together
in time to music.

4. Boys sit on hands, and with legs crossed, rock to left and right.

5. Boys sit on hands and crack toes together in time to music.

6. Boys swing feet alternately, hitting wall in time to music.

7. Boys suddenly roll over on stomachs, and swing feet alternately.

8. Boys crack feet together in time to music.

9. Boys roll over, one after another, and sit up looking over the edge of the wall and shaking heads dubiously.

10. Boys rise and stand on wall, marking time to music with feet.

11. Boys gradually lie down with feet toward rear of wall.

12. Boys peep over the wall, shaking heads from left to right.

13. Boys stand and face each other by twos.

14. They peep over the wall and shake heads and fingers dubiously.

15. Each alternate boy, beginning with head boy, sits down on the wall, and holds hand up to partner, who peeps over dubiously.

16. Boys standing put their hands under their partners' arms and pull them back. Boys rise.

17. Boys all swing their arms as though pre-

paring to dive, and suddenly sit "plump" down on wall.

18. Each alternate boy, as in 15, rises, swings arms and leaps off into the hay.

19. Boys who are down reach hands up to partners. These boys roll over on stomachs, and gradually drop down the wall, with or without partner's assistance.

20. Boys run about stage and gather in a line near footlights.

21. Bow to audience several times.

22. Line follows leader and runs toward rear of the stage in a zigzag line. Here they separate gradually, some running behind wall at right and some at left.

23. Boys clamber up wall from rear, with cheers and waving of hats. As last boy appears the curtain drops on the hilarious return of Humpty-Dumpty.

Uncle Tom's Cabin

DRAMATIS PERSONÆ

TOPSY.

EVA.

MISS OPHELIA.

SCENE FROM UNCLE TOM'S CABIN.

Scene—Miss Ophelia's bedroom: Door to the *left*: at the back in centre a bed, or couch arranged as bed, standing out from the wall; to the *right* side of the bed, a dressing-table: on it, besides the usual looking-glass, etc., a bright red ribbon and a pair of white gloves. Chair to *right* near front of stage. Book-case, pictures, and other furniture, according to convenience. When the curtain rises, Miss Ophelia is discovered sitting on chair to *right*: opposite to her stands Topsy, hands folded, eyes fixed on the ground.

Miss Ophelia—Now Topsy, you are clean and tidy at last, I hope?

Topsy—Laws, yes, Miss Feely! There's not a speck o' dirt left on me.

Miss Ophelia—That is better: I hope you will always keep clean and tidy in the future. There is nothing I dislike so much as dirt.

Topsy (rolling her eyes and making a face)— Yes, missis.

Miss Ophelia Now I have a few questions to

ask you before we set to work. How old are you, Topsy?

Topsy (grinning)—Dunno, missis.

Miss Ophelia—Don't know how old you are! Did nobody ever tell you? Who was your mother then, child?

Topsy (with another grin)—Never had none.

Miss Ophelia Never had any mother! What do you mean? Where were you born?

Topsy—Never was born.

Miss Ophelia (sternly)—You musn't answer me like that, child. I am not playing with you. Tell me where you were born and who were your father and mother.

Topsy (emphatically)—Never was born, never had no father, nor mother, nor nothin'!

Miss Ophelia—Topsy, how can you say such things! How long have you lived with your master and mistress?

Topsy—Dunno, missis.

Miss Ophelia—Is it a year, or more, or less? Try to answer properly, this time.

Topsy—Dunno missis.

Miss Ophelia—Worse and worse! Do you know anything at all, I wonder! Have you ever heard of God, Topsy? (Topsy shakes her head.) Do you know who made you?

Topsy—(laughing)—Nobody as I knows on: 'spect I grow'd. Don't think nobody ever made me.

Miss Ophelia (shocked)—Terrible! whatever shall I do with a child like this! Do you know how to sew, Topsy?

Topsy—No, missis.

Miss Ophelia—What can you do? What did you do for your master and mistress?

Topsy—Fetch water, wash dishes, and clean knives and wait on folks.

Miss Ophelia (going to left side of bed)—Well now, Topsy, I'm going to show you just how my bed is to be made. I am very particular about my bed. You must learn exactly how to do it. Come to the other side and watch me well.

Topsy (going to *right* side)—Yes, ma'am.

Miss Ophelia Now, Topsy, look here. This is the hem of the sheet. This is the right side of the sheet. This is the wrong. Will you remember?

Topsy (with a big sigh)—Yes, ma'am.

Miss Ophelia—Well now, the undersheet you must bring over—like this—and tuck it right down under the mattress, nice and smooth—like this. Do you see?

Topsy (with a bigger sigh)—Yes, ma'am.

Miss Ophelia—But the upper sheet must be brought down and tucked under, firm and smooth at the foot—like this—the narrow hem at the foot.

Topsy (snatching the gloves and the ribbon off the dressing-table, as Miss Ophelia bends over the bed)—Yes ma'am. (*Slips them into her sleeve.*)

Miss Ophelia (pulling off the clothes again)—Now, Topsey, let me see if you can do it. (Topsy quickly and neatly makes the bed again.)

Miss Ophelia (watching her)—Very good . . very good indeed, Topsy! We shall make something of you yet.

Topsy (tucking in the sheet)—Yes, missis. (As she does so the ribbon falls from her sleeve.)

Miss Ophelia (picking it up)—What is this? You naughty wicked child, you have been stealing!

Topsy (very surprised)—Why! That's Miss Feely's ribbon, ain't it? How could it a' got into my sleeve?

Miss Ophelia—Topsy, you naughty girl, don't tell me a lie. You stole that ribbon.

Topsy—Missis, I declare I didn't. Never seed it till dis blessed minnit.

Miss Ophelia—Topsy, don't you know it is wicked to tell lies?

Topsy—I never tell no lies, Miss Feely. It's jist the truth I've been tellin' now. It an't nothin' else.

Miss Ophelia—Topsy, I shall have to whip you if you tell lies so.

Topsy (beginning to cry)—Laws, missis, if you whips all day couldn't say no other way. I never seed that ribbon. It must a' caught in my sleeve. Miss Feely must a' left it on the bed, and it got caught in the clothes, and so got in my sleeve.

Miss Ophelia (angrily shaking her)—Topsy, how dare you! Don't you tell me that again. (*The gloves fall to the ground.*)

Miss Ophelia (holding them up)—There! Will you tell me you didn't steal the ribbon?

Topsy (still crying loudly)—O missis, missis, I'se so sorry! I won't never do it again, I won't.

Miss Ophelia—Stop crying then, and tell me if you have taken anything else since you have been in the house. If you tell me truthfully, I won't whip you.

Topsy—Laws, missis, I took Miss Eva's red thing she wears on her neck.

Miss Ophelia—You did, you naughty child! Go and bring it me this minute.

Topsy—Laws, missis, I can't—they's burnt up.

Miss Ophelia—Burnt up? What a story! Go and get them or I shall whip you.

Topsy (groaning and crying)—I can't, I can't Miss Feely! They's burnt up, they is.

Miss Ophelia—What did you burn them up for?

Topsy (rocking to and fro)—'Cause I'se wicked, I is. I'se mighty wicked. I can't help it. (Enter Eva wearing red necklace.)

Miss Ophelia—Why, Eva, where did you get your red necklace?

Eva—Get it? Why, I have had it on all day, and what is funny, aunty, I had it on all night. I forgot to take it off when I went to bed.

Miss Ophelia (lifting her hands in despair)— What ever shall I do with her! What in the world made you tell me that you took the necklace, Topsy?

Topsy (wiping her eyes)—Missis said I must 'fess. I couldn't think of nothin' else to 'fess.

Miss Ophelia—But of course I didn't want you to confess things you didn't do; that is telling a lie just as much as the other.

Topsy (very surprised)—Laws now, is it?

What in the world made you tell me that you took the necklace, Topsy?—Page 37

Miss Ophelia—Topsy, what makes you behave so badly?

Topsy (grinning)—Dunno, missis; 'spects it's my wicked heart.

Miss Ophelia—What shall I do with you?   I'm sure I don't know; this is terrible.

Topsy—Laws, missis, you must whip me.   I an't used to workin' unless I gets whipped, but I dunno that it helps much neither.   My old missis, she whipped me hard an' pulled my hair, and knocked my head agin the door, but it did'nt do me no good.   I 'spect if they was to pull every hair out o' my head it would'nt do no good neither.   I'se so wicked.   I'se nothin' but a nigger.

Miss Ophelia (going to door)—I never saw such a child!   Topsy, if you do not try to be more honest, and better in everyway, I shall have to speak to your master.   *(exit.)*

Eva—What makes you so naughty, Topsy? Why don't you try to be good? *(taking her hand.)*   Don't you love anybody, Topsy?

Topsy (blinking her eyes)—Dunno nothin' 'bout love.   I love candy, that's all.

Eva—But you love your father and mother?

Topsy—Never had none: I telled ye that before, Miss Eva.

Eva (sadly)—Oh, I forgot: but hadn't you any brother or sister, or aunt, or . . .

Topsy (interrupting)—No, none on 'em. Never had nothin' nor nobody.

Eva—But, Topsy, if you would only try to be good, you might . . .

Topsy (interrupting)—Couldn't never be nothin' but a nigger, if I was ever so good. If I could come white, I'd try then.

Eva—But people can love you, if you are black, Topsy. Miss Ophelia would love you if you were good.

Topsy (laughing)—Would she though?

Eva—Don't you think so?

Topsy—She can't bear me, 'cause I'm a nigger. She'd as soon have a toad touch her. There can't nobody love niggers, and niggers can't do nothin.' I don't care. (*Whistles or hums, and tosses her head.*)

Eva (laying her hand on Topsy's shoulder)— O Topsy, I will love you: I love you now, because you haven't any mother or father or friends; because you have been beaten and starved and ill-used. I love you, and I want you to be good. It makes me sorry to have you so naughty. I wish you would try to be good,

Topsy. Won't you? (Topsy suddenly sits down on the floor and cries softly, hiding her face in her apron.)

Eva (stroking her head)—Poor Topsy!

Topsy—O Miss Eva, dear Miss Eva, I will try . . . indeed I will. I never did care nothin' about it before.

CURTAIN.

In Birdland

IN BIRDLAND.

All.

O Birdland is a busy place,
  Where many trades abound
And many little workers skilled,
  Within its realms are found.

Upon the earth—on which we dwell—
  All men must work to live,
To "arts and crafts" and many trades
  Their time and strength they give.

And so it is in Birdland, too,
  No idlers there, no drones—
Where hearts are light, and songs are sung
  In merry, joyous tones.

Child (showing a picture of the tailor bird and its curious-
ly-fashioned nest).

Here is the little tailor bird,
  Who sews wee leaves together,
And fashions, thus, a cosy nest
  For wet or sunny weather.

Child (showing a picture of the Baltimore oriole and its nest).

As the oriole builds a new nest each year, a discarded nest is not hard to discover, suspended from the tip of the swaying branch of an elm tree, although it may be difficult to reach.)

The oriole gay, doth weave a nest
Of soft threads to and fro,
And hangs it where 'twill gently swing
When'er light breezes blow.

Orioles (two children out of sight of the class, sing)

Oriole song.

(Melody: "Rock-a-bye Baby")

The rain may fall,
The wind may blow,
Safe is our nest
As it swings to and fro.

Up in the elm tree,
Swinging you see,
Safe from danger,
Ever are we.

Child (showing a picture of the barn swallow, and, if possible, a picture of a barn with the swallows in sight)

The swallow small a mason is,
　He takes both mud and leaves
To build his house, and plaster it,
　Beneath the sloping eaves.

Child (showing a picture of the woodpecker, and, if possible, the picture of a tree with his "hole," or nest, in it)

The woodpecker a hole doth find
　Within an aged tree,
And bores, just like a carpenter,
　To make it deep, you see.

(As a "tap, tap tap," is heard from an unseen quarter of the room.)

There's a rap-a-tap-tap
　In the tall cherry tree,
'Tis a queer little sound.
　O what can it be?

It sounds like a cobbler
　With hammer and awl;
Or is it a visitor
　Coming to call?

(Child who has been "tapping" for the woodpecker comes into view.)

Oho, busy woodpecker!
So 'tis no one but you,
With your "rap-a-tap-tap"
Meaning, *"How do you do?"*

Oho, gay Woodpecker!
You are busy, you say,
Boring a hall
To your new house to-day?

Well, work away fast,
With your queer little awl!
A carpenter's known
By the chips he lets fall.

Child (showing a picture of a robin and its nest—if possible, a real nest.)

Just like a potter at his wheel—
With clay, and hair, and straw—
The robin shapes his bowl-like nest,
Without a break or flaw.

Child (showing a picture of an oven bird, and, if possible, one also of a nest).

A baker, sure, this bird should be—
Since he an oven makes—
Yet, I have never, never heard
He pies or cookies bakes.

Child (showing the picture of a chimney-swift).

With patient skill, the chimney-swift
A twig-like basket forms,
And glues it in the chimney place,
Safe sheltered from the storms.

Child (showing a picture of the bank swallows, and, if possible, of a river bank with the holes or trenches, to the nests in view).

The bank swallows dig with beak and claws—
They must wee miners be;
For often—'long a river bank—
Their tunnels you may see.

All.

O Birdland is a wondrous place,
Where with its tiny feet and bill,
Each little bird, with instinct keen,
Its dainty nest can build with skill.

It matters not where each may be,
In orchard, field, or leafy wood,
The father bird and mother bird
Soon hatch and rear a baby brood.

O dreary place would be this world,
Were there no birds to chirp and sing,
For Birdland music thrills the heart,
Into each life fresh joy doth bring.

The Ladder of Gold

THE LADDER OF GOLD.

SCENE—A darkened room across which falls a shaft of light. This may be secured by placing a lamp high on the wall and allowing its rays to fall through a hole in a dark curtain. A lantern slide of Reynolds' "Angels' Heads" may be used effectively.

Two children are discovered playing with letter blocks on the floor. Suddenly Millie's attention is caught by the ray of light.

Millie (aged 10)—Oh! Fred, there's the ladder of gold Mama told us about.

Fred (aged 6)—Hm! That's only the light coming through the window blinds.

Millie—That's what you call it, but that's the way it comes; and Mama said it was a ladder of gold let down from the sky when the sun was tired and going to bed.

Fred—I know Mama said so, but I think it is only a chink in the window shutter.

Millie—And I think it is a golden ladder, because Mama said so. She told us it rests on the floor, a little round island of gold, (pointing to the floor) and there it is.

Fred—Yes, that's so.

Millie—And that if we looked at it steadily, a few minutes, we could see moving up and down the ladder, little angels' heads with wings, all in a row.

Fred—I don't see any, do you?   (gazing intently.)

Millie—Not yet, but we will if we keep looking, I'm sure.

Fred—Heads with wings?

Millie—Yes, like beads upon strings, Mama said, or like faces peeping out of the bed-clothes.

Fred (moving toward the shaft of light —I think I see one.   There!

Millie—Oh! Fred so do I.   Yes, two—three— there and there!   But you must not try to catch them!   You would only frighten them away.

Fred—Millie, where do you think they come from?

Millie—Mama says they're ideal things, and all ideal things come right down from the sky.

Fred—You think they live in the sky?

Millie—Yes, and once when they came they stayed long enough to have their portraits painted by one of the great painters of old, which Mama showed me in a book.

Fred—I should think then that he would have talked with them.

Millie.

Oh! he did and they told him:
From their home in the skies,
Where none ever dies,
Their ladder to earth is let down;
And these little elves come
To visit our home,
And the children who live in the town.
Don't you remember, Fred?

Fred.

Yes.
How they laugh and they sing,
As they drift on the wing,
Down their ladder of gold dust and pearl
"Oh! children, be good!
Be good! Be good!"
They sing to each boy and each girl.

Millie.

They do not stay long,
To finish their song,
When once their mission is told
But upward they fly,
These wights of the sky,
And carry their ladder of gold.

Fred.

And all the long day,
From far, far away,
These sweet little strangers have come;
So up through the bars
To the pavement of stars
They make their way back again home.

Millie.

And these dear little heads,
Go away to their beds
In cloudland far up in the sky;
But some other night,
With their ladder of light,
They will come if the children don't cry.

Robin Hood

DRAMATIS PERSONÆ

KING RICHARD CŒUR DE LION.
Three Nobles, attendants on him.
ROBIN HOOD.
LITTLE JOHN.
MUCH.
ALLAN-A-DALE.
FRIAR TUCK.
Robin Hood's Merry Men.
MAID MARIAN.
LADY CHRISTABEL.

ROBIN HOOD.

SCENE—An open space in Sherwood Forest.
To the *Right* and *Left,* trees or greenery; at the
back a bank. When the curtain rises King Richard is discovered standing in centre; near him the
three Nobles. They are all dressed in monks'
cloaks, with hoods well drawn over their faces.

The King (looking round him)—Well! I
hope we shall see the fellow this time.

First Noble—There is not much fear of that:
Robin Hood finds out monks as quickly as bees
do honey. We shall not have long to wait, your
Majesty.

The King (softly, putting finger on lip)—
Hush! He may be listening now, and if he
guesses who I am our game is spoilt. Remember I am only an abbot for to-day. (*louder*)
The fellow is well off here: sunshine and green
trees, flowers and the song of the birds for company—who could want more?

Second Noble (speaking quickly)—I saw
something move down there . . . through the
trees . . . take care, my Lord!

The King (still loudly)—For my part, I have no fear of the man. He would not dare rob *me*.

Robin Hood (stepping from behind a tree, all in green, with bow and arrow, and horn)—You speak too soon, my lord abbot—for an abbot I take you to be by your dress and manner. Robin Hood dare rob whom he will, when he has need of money, so you had better come with me peacefully. I have a hundred men within call, and I am not over fond of monks.

The King—If we are monks, we are also messengers from the King. If you are the famous Robin Hood . . .

Robin Hood—I am Robin Hood.

The King—Then his Majesty sent us to say that he would see you. As a sign he sends you this ring (*showing ring on his hand*).

Robin Hood (after looking at it, taking off his hat)—It is truly the King's ring. God bless him: God bless all those that love him: cursed be all those who hate him and rebel against him.

The King—Then you curse yourself, for you are a traitor and an outlaw.

Robin Hood (fiercely)—I am an outlaw may be, through no fault of mine, but I am no traitor, and if you were not the messenger of the King you would pay dearly for that lie. I have never yet hurt any true and honest man: I have robbed only from the tyrant rich, never from the poor: I fight against monks and abbots, and take their money from them when I can, because they steal from the poor. They ought to live good lives and show others a good example, but they do not. They live wickedly, and should be punished. If they had ruled England well when King Richard was away, we should not have to live in the woods as we do now. (*kindly.*) But do not fear, you are the King's messengers, and therefore welcome to all that we have. Stay here, and sup with us; we will make you comfortable as we know how.

Third Noble—They wait for us at Nottingham, my lord.

The King—Let them wait: the King wishes to know as much as possible about this man. If we do not fare well, it will matter not for once.

Robin Hood—You shall eat of our best, Sir Abbot, though if you came not from the King I doubt if you would be so well treated. (blows his horn. Enter quickly, Little John, Much, Allan-A-Dale, and others: they are all dressed in green.)

Little John—What news, master?

Robin Hood—None that will fill our pockets,

my little John. These good monks are messengers from the King, and therefore safe from us. Much!

Much—Yes, master!

Robin Hood—. . . Tell the cook that we shall dine here, and that we must have as fine a feast as if the King himself were among us.

Much—Yes, master! (*Goes out by* Left *quickly.*)

Robin Hood—Allan-a-dale, go bring me here Maid Marian, and your sweet Christabel; tell them we have need of their help to entertain our noble company.

Allan-A-Dale—I go right gladly, master.

(exit by *Left.*)

Robin Hood (to the others)—Now, men, help bring the things and do your parts with a right good will. Let us show these gentlemen what we poor foresters can do.

All—Ay, that we will, master!

(Exit all foresters, save Little John. They all drop on one knee before Robin as they pass out.)

The King—Upon my word, Sir Outlaw, you are master of a gallant company. It is a pity that you should live as you do—shooting down the King's deer, robbing his faithful bishops and knights.

Robin Hood—I cannot starve my men, Sir Abbot, and were Richard himself here I think he would scarcely grudge these fine men their food.

The King—Perchance not, but it is against the law.

Robin Hood—I know that well, Sir Abbot, but what else can we do? Our homes have been burned down by the Norman nobles, our lands have been stolen, our money taken, and they would have made us their slaves. Rather than that, we have chosen to live here in the merry greenwood. We are Englishmen, Sir Monk, and we would be free.

The King—Well spoken! Well defended, Robin! (Enter by *Left* Allan-A-Dale , with Maid Marian, Lady Christabel, and Friar Tuck.)

Maid Marian (curtsying)—Welcome to Sherwood Forest, Sir Abbot!

The King—Who is this fair lady?

Friar Tuck (pushing forward)—Have you never heard of Maid Marian, Robin Hood's sweet bride, and Queen of our merry greenwood? She comes of noble blood, but rather than be parted from her Robin she fled to the forest all in knightly array. There she again met our master, and the two young things fell to fighting to-

gether, neither knowing the other; presently
Robin spoke and the lady discovered herself, and
the end of it all was that I married them myself.
Ah, it was a merry wedding!

The King—Who is this jolly monk?

Friar Tuck—Friar Tuck, at your service, my
lord abbot, and a very busy man.   Look at these
two. (*pointing to* Allan-A-Dale *and the* Lady
Christabel).   I married them under the old
bishop's nose: I cried them seven times in the
church lest there should be some mistake.   They
are a couple to be proud of.   They . . .

Robin Hood—Friar Tuck, Friar Tuck, your
tongue clacks too loudly.

Friar Tuck—Not so, master, not so; you would
be badly off without its clacking, I'll warrant.
Who would marry you?   Who would bless you?
Who would say grace at meat in the Latin
tongue?   Who would . . . (Little John takes
him by the arm and leads him away.)

Robin Hood (laughing)—He is a merry soul!

(Enter a Page ⌈or Pages⌉ with silver or crystal bowl and
towel. He kneels before the King, holding the bowl while he
washes his hands, then goes to the Nobles. Men in green
come hurrying in with mugs, platters, dishes, food, etc., which
they set on the grass. Little John orders them here and there:
the King and Nobles talk to Maid Marian and Christabel.
Presently Robin Hood blows his horn: all the men stand
round.)

Robin Hood—Fill up the mugs, men, to the very brim: before we eat we will drink the King's health. (They fill up mugs, giving them also to the King and Nobles.)

All drinking (*led by Robin Hood*)—God save the King !

The King—If I could get you pardon from the King, Robin, would you be willing to leave this wild life in the woods and serve him for ever? He has need of loyal and true men like you.

Robin Hood—With all my heart!

The King (to the men)—Men, would you be willing to serve the King of England, Richard Cœur de Lion?

All (flinging their caps into the air)—With all our hearts! . . . God save the King!

Robin Hood—You see, Sir Abbot, we are all loyal people here.

The King (huskily)—So I see!

Robin Hood—If you would but ask the King to forgive me, I think I could once more respect monks. A bishop was the first cause of all our misfortunes, and because of that I have hated them all, but from this day I shall respect them.

The King (flinging back the monk's hood)— There is no need to ask the King for pardon.

I am the King your sovereign, and I forgive you gladly, Robin.

Robin Hood (falling on his knees)—O Sire!

The King—Stand up, stand up, my friend: I doubt, if in all England, I have more faithful followers than you and your men.

Little John—The King! God save us! . . . The King!!

Much and others—The King! The King! (*they all kneel*).

The King—Rise, all! I am King Richard of England: are you ready to follow me as your master, and be my men?

All—We are, we are!

The King (gaily)—Then let us sup, and after we will to Nottingham, and surprise them.

All—Long live the King! Three cheers for Cœur de Lion! And three for Robin Hood!

(The King gives his hand to Maid Marian, Robin Hood to Christabel. As they all seat themselves round the feast the curtain falls.)

DRAMATIS PERSONÆ

Abou Cassim (a rich merchant).
Zuleika
Ayesha
Fatima
Prince Furryskin.
Molinko (his servant).

BEAUTY AND THE BEAST.

A Romantic Drama for Children, in Six Scenes.

SCENE *1.—About Cassim's house. Zu. and Ay. writing at different tables.*

Zul.—What are you writing, sister Ayesha?

Ay.—I'm making a list of all the things I want father to buy me when he is away. What are you writing, sister Zuleika?

Zul.—I'm doing the same thing—but it is so tiresome, I can't remember any of the things I want.

Ay.—Can't you? poor thing! I can. I've put down twenty-nine things on my list.

Zul.—Twenty-nine? dear me! and I have only seventeen on mine! It is hardly worth while making a list at all!

> [*Abou Cassim heard calling outside.*

Ab. C.—Zuleika, Ayesha, Fatima!

Zul. and Ay.—Yes, father.

Enter Abou Cassim, still calling.

Ab. C.—Zuleika—Ayesha—Fatima! where is

everybody? why don't you answer when you are
called? why don't you come and help me to pack
my things?

Zul.—Oh, father, I am so sorry. I was just
coming.

Ab. C.—Just coming—what's the good of
that? I'm just going! you'll make me miss my
camel! I said he was to be at the door at 3
o'clock, and it is now——[*Looks at the sun.*] I
never can remember where the sun ought to be
in the afternoon. I wish people used watches in
Turkey.

Ay.—Oh, father, some day you must go a long
way across the sea, to buy me a real gold watch,
like the one you told me about once.

Ab. C.—I dare say! you think that your father
has nothing to do but go shopping for you!
Where is Fatima, my dear youngest girl? she is
the only one that is any use to me when I am
starting on my travels. Fatima—Beauty!

[*Goes up, C.*

Zul. (to Ay)—It makes me sick to hear her
called Beauty.

Ay.—So it does me. She's no more a beauty
than we are!

Zul.—Not half so much.

Enter Fatima—she throws herself into Abou Cassim's arms.

Fat.—Dear, dear father! I wish you were not going away.

Ab. C.—Yes, my darling, so do I—never mind, I shall soon be back again.

Fat.—I've packed all your things, father, and got everything ready.

Ab. C.—There's a good little girl. [*Comes forward.*] Now, am I to bring you anything back this time?

Zul. and Ay.—Oh, yes, father!

Ab. C.—What would you like?

Zul. and Ay. (unrolling lists).—We've made a list.

Ab. C. (horrified).—Made a list—upon my word, you have! You don't expect me to bring back all those things, do you? Why, I should have to buy two extra camels and three ostriches, to carry the parcels across the desert.

Zul.—Oh, but I assure you, father, they are things we really want.

Ay.—That we couldn't possibly do without.

Zul. (reads).—An embroidered sash——

Ay (reads).—A pair of golden slippers——

Zul—A silk veil——

Ay.—A new turban——

Zul.—Some diamond earrings——

Ay.—A new-fashioned skirt——

Zul.—Some spangled muslin——

Ay.—A tame monkey——

Zul.—A box of sweetmeats——

Ay.—A white ass——

Zul.—A gold necklace——

Ay.—A tall turban——

Ab. C.—Stop, stop! here, give me the lists, and if I can I will bring you each a present. (To Fat.)   And what would you like, my darling?

Fat.—Oh, father dear, if you only come back safe I want nothing else.

Zul. (aside).—Little humbug!

Ab. C.—What, nothing at all?

Fat.—Well then, bring me a rose—just one beautiful rose—nothing more.

Ab. C.—A red rose—very well, I will bring it.   Goodbye then, my children.

[*Fat. dries her eyes—Zul. and Ay. crying loudly.*

Ab. C.—Why, what a fuss about nothing!   Is a man never to go away from home on business without having all his womankind boohooing like this?

Zul.—Oh, father, we're so afraid!

Ab. C.—Afraid of what? that I shall be lost in the desert?

Zul.—No—that you will forget some of our commissions!

Ab. C.—Nonsense!   I must be off.

Fat.—Take care of yourself, dear father.

Zul.—Don't mount your camel till he is kneeling.

Ay.—And don't fall off as he gets up again.

Finale.   Tune—'My Maryland.'

Fat.—Oh, come back to your daughters soon, dear papa, oh, dear papa.

Ay.—We don't like being left alone, dear papa, oh, dear papa.

Zul.—When you are gone, we cry all day.

We don't know what to do or say.

Zul., Ay., and Fat.—We wish you would not go away, dear papa, oh, dear papa.

Ab. C.—I'm sorry thus to cause you pain, your dear papa, your dear papa.

I'll soon come back to you again, your dear papa, your dear papa.

But I'm a merchant, as you know,

And that is why I travel so.

I buy and sell, I come and go, your dear papa, your dear papa.

[*Exit Abou Cassim. Zul., Ay., Fat. sitting in a row—Zul. R.—Fat. C.—Ay. L.*

Fat.—Oh dear, I wish father were not gone.

Zul.—Well, it is no use wishing—what shall we do to amuse ourselves?

Ay.—Shall we go out?

Zul.—I don't care about going out—shall we stay in?

Fat.—I don't care about staying in, unless we do something.　Shall we make toffee?

Ay.—I don't care about making toffee.　Shall we blow soap bubbles?

Zul.—I don't care about blowing soap bubbles. Shall we paint?

Fat.—I don't care about painting.　[*All sit silent.*

Ay.—I have an idea.

Zul. and Fat.—What?

Ay.—Let us dance!　　　　[*All clap hands.*

Zul.—Oh yes!

Zul.—Oh yes!

Fat.—Do let us dance!　　　　　[*All dance.*

Curtain.

SCENE *II.—Prince   Furryskin's   garden.
Prince alone.*

Pr.—Dear me—how tiresome it is to be a beast!
especially for a person who really ought to be a
beautiful young prince, dressed in blue and silver,
instead of having this horrid hairy skin on.   I
wish a wicked fairy had not enchanted me at my
birth! it is very inconvenient.   And the worst of
it is, that I shall never turn into a young prince
again until a beautiful girl tells me she loves me
—as if I were likely that a beautiful girl would
say anything of the kind to me!   Well, well—it
can't be helped, I suppose—I must try and
amuse myself with my flowers, and see if I can't
forget how ugly and hairy I am.   [*Walks
about.*]   My pinks are looking very nice, certainly, and my Canterbury bells—and my dah-
lias are pretty good—but my roses have been very
bad this year.   However, I see there is one red
rose on my favorite tree--I must tell the gardener
not to gather it, I like seeing it grow on the tree
best.   This is certainly a very nice garden, and
if I were not a beast I should enjoy it very much.

[*Gathers a pink.   Strolls off, R.*

Enter Abou Cassim, carrying bundles.

Ab. C.—Now I really think I have got as many things for those girls as I can well carry— I had to leave the rest in the desert. The only thing I have not yet got is the rose that Beauty asked me for—I came through this beautiful garden in hopes of finding one. Ha— there is exactly what I want.

Enter Prince, R. Ab. C. gathers rose. Pr. rushes at him.

Pr.—Wretch! [*Seizes him by the collar. Ab. C. drops rose*] Who are you, who dare to pluck my favorite rose?

Ab. C.—I'm very sorry, I'm sure—I did not know it was your rose.

Pr.—But you knew it wasn't yours, I suppose?

Ab. C.—Well, yes—I must confess I did.

Pr.—Then if you knew it wasn't yours, you knew that you were stealing—and if you were stealing, you are a thief—and if you are a thief, you must have your head cut off!

Ab. C.—Oh, sir—pray don't cut off my head —I couldn't see my way home if you did.

Pr.—See your way home? don't you wish you may get there? Do you know who I am?

Ab. C.—I really can't say—I think I've seen some one very like you before, but perhaps it was at the Zoo. Are you a bear very like a man, or a man very like a bear?

Pr.—Never you mind which—it is just the same to you, as I'm going to kill you and eat you in about a minute and a half. Taking my rose that I loved so!

Ab. C.—Oh, your lordship—your beastship, I mean—it was not for myself I took the rose—I took it for my daughter, my youngest daughter, Beauty, whom I love more dearly than you love your flowers.

Pr. (starts).—Your daughter, did you say? Is she beautiful at all?

Ab. C.—Very, very beautiful—she is considered particularly like her father.

Pr.—Oh—indeed—she must be a beauty then! What will you give me if I spare your worthless life?

Ab. C.—Anything you like to ask.

Pr.—Well—promise to give me the first living thing you meet when you get inside your garden, and I will let you go free.

Ab. C. (kneeling.)—Oh, most generous beast! how can I thank you?

Pr.—By getting up and taking yourself off, and not making marks on my gravel path. I'm very particular about my garden, as you may have observed.

Duet—Finale.

Pr.—Now please walk out at my garden gate—
You'll find it is better for you not to wait,
In case I might take such a fancy to you
I might gobble you up in a minute or two,
And then of you there'd be nothing more,
So I think you had better get out of the door.
    Ab C.—Very well, I'll walk out of your garden gate—
I think it is better for me not to wait,
In case you might take such a fancy to me
You might gobble me up in a minute or three,
And then of me there'd be nothing more,
So I think I had better get out of the door.

Curtain.

Scene *III—Outside Abou Cassim's house.*

Ab. C.—Not a dog or a cat to be seen! I promised that Beast, or Prince, or whatever he calls himself to send him the first living thing I met on my way home—and I haven't seen so much as a spider since I got inside the gate!

[Beauty runs out.

Fat. Dear, dear father! how glad I am to see you!

Ab. C.—Fatima, my child—alas! alas!

Fat.—Why father, are not you glad to see me? And I have been watching for you every day from the top of the house! and you've got my rose, too! thank you so much.

[Smells it.

Zul. and Ay.—Oh, father! is it you? Have you brought our things?

Ab. C.—I got them, yes—but there were so many of them that the camel who carried them died of fatigue in crossing the desert, and the eagles ate the camel and the parcels too—and so I have nothing.

Zul.—Oh, father! how could you?

Ay.—How couldn't you? *[Both sob.*

Ab. C.—Parcels, indeed—as if that were all that we have to care about. There's worse than that, I can tell you. I have—I have—— *[Sobs loudly.*

Zul., Ay., Fat.—What, father, what?

Ab. C.—I have sold my daughter to a beast!

Zul.—Your daughter, which?

Ab. C. (covers his face with his hands and points to Fatima).—That one!

Zul. and Ay.—Thank goodness!

[*Fat. falls into her father's arms.*

Curtain.

Scene *IV—Prince Furryskin's dining-room.*

Pr. (calls.)—Molinko! Molinko! Where is that boy gone? I never knew such a tiresome servant! Molinko!

Mol. (behind.)—What's the matter now?

Pr. Come here, directly.

Enter Molinko.

Mol.—Well, here I am.

Pr.—Didn't you hear me calling you?

Mol.—Of course I did.

Pr.—Then why didn't you come?

Mol.—Because I was waiting till you left off.

Pr.—Have you done all the things I told you?

Mol.—No.

Pr.—Didn't I tell you that I dreamt the merchant would bring his beautiful daughter here to-day? and that you were to get everything ready?

Mol.—Yes.

Pr.—And is it ready?

Mol.—No.

Pr.—Why not?

Mol.—Because it isn't.

Pr.—Now listen—you are to put lovely flowers in her room—silken sheets on her bed—embroidered curtains to her windows—all the most beautiful things you can think of.   Do you hear?

Mol.—Yes.

Pr.—And the dinner must be lovely too—all kinds of nice things to eat—sweetmeats—raisins —jam—fruits—chocolate——

Mol.—Yes.

Pr.—And lay the table for two—I will dine with her.   [*Exit Prince.*

Mol. (alone.)   [*Lays Table.*]   Why, there's nothing but work from morning till night here!

Song.   Tune—'So Early in the Morning.'

I have to work so hard all day,
That I have never time to play—
I'm butler, groom, and housemaid too,
I've got too much hard work to do.
From early in the morning,
From early in the morning,

From early in the morning,
Until the break of day.

Enter Fatima—looks round.

Fat.—I thought I heard singing—was that you?

Mol.—Yes.

Fat.—And who are you?

Mol.—I'm Molinko, the Prince's servant. And who are you?

Fat.—I'm Fatima, Abou Cassim's daughter.

Mol.—Then you're the lady who is coming to dinner?

Fat.—I suppose so—is it ready?

Mol.—No, it isn't—nothing's ready.

Fat.—Nothing?

Mol.—No, nothing—your bed isn't—nor your room, nor your curtains, nor your silk sheets, nor anything! so now!

Fat.—Well, well— don't be angry—I don't mind.

Mol.—That's a good thing.

　　　　[*Repeats song—Fat. joins in chorus.*

Mol.—I'll go and tell my master you are here.

　　　　　　　　[*Exit. Mol.*

Fat.—Alas—how strange to be here, away

from all those I love.   I wonder what they are doing in my home, my dear old home?

Song.

Mid pleasures and palaces though we may roam,
Be it ever so humble, there's no place like home.
A charm from the skies seems to hallow us there,
Which seek through the world is ne'er met with
    elsewhere;
    Home, home, sweet, sweet home;
Be it ever so humble there's no place like home.

Enter Prince.   Fatima starts up.

Pr.—Don't be frightened!   I'm not dangerous.

Fat.—Are you sure?

Pr.—Quite.   Beautiful damsel, are you Abou Cassim's daughter?

Fat.   I am—his youngest daughter.

Pr.—His beloved daughter Beauty, of whom he spoke?

Fat.—The same.

Pr.—He is right to call you Beauty—you are very beautiful.

Fat.   I'm glad you think so.

Pr.—But alas—I will not ask you if you think me beautiful.

Fat.—No, I wouldn't if I were you.

Pr.—Am I too ugly for you to dine with me?

Fat.—Not if you have nice things for dinner.

Pr.—You shall have the best of everything I can give you. Here Molinko!

Mol. (behind).—Yes!

Pr.—Be quick, lazy bones!

Enter Mol.

Mol.—I'm being as quick as I can, long claws!

Pr. (to Fat).—What may I give you—some Turkish delight?

Fat.—Please.

Pr.— Oh, how Turkish delightful it is to see you eat it! Have some lemonade?

Fat.—Please.   [*They drink. Prince sings.*

Song.

Drink to me only with thine eyes,
    And I will pledge with mine—
Or leave a kiss within the cup,
    And I'll not ask for wine.
The thirst that from the soul doth spring,
    Doth ask a drink divine—
But might I of Jove's nectar sip,
    I would not change with thine.

Pr.—Beauty, you like me better now, don't you?

Fat.—Oh, yes, much!

Pr.—Do you think you could say you loved me?

Fat.—Oh no—certainly not. Now I should like to go back to my father again, please.

Pr.—What, and leave me?

Fat.—Yes, please.

Pr.—Then I shall die of grief.

Fat.—Oh, no, you won't.

Pr.—You shall do as you like, Fatima, you shall not think me unkind as well as ugly—but first would you like to take a turn round the garden, and see if I can find another rose for you?

Fat.—Yes, please.   [*Exeunt.*

Curtain.

Scene *V.*—*Same as Scene 1.   Abou Cassim's drawing-room.   Zul. R—Fat., Ay., Ab C. L. Smoking and reading.*

Zul.—Well, Beauty—well? tell us all about it.

Ay.—What is the beast like?

Fat.—He was very nice and kind.

Zul.—But what was he like to look at, I mean?

Fat.—He is all over hair—and he has great

furry ears, and I dare say he has claws too, but
I didn't see them.

Ay.—And what did you have for dinner?

Fat.—Oh, all kinds of nice things.

Zul.—I do wish we had been there! why didn't
you stay, you silly girl?

Fat.—Because I wanted to come back and see
you all again.

Ab. C.—Good girl, Beauty, very good girl,
she likes her home best—that's what all good girls
do.

Ay.—And didn't he give you any presents?

Ab. C.—You think of nothing but presents.

Fat.—Yes, he gave me this looking-glass.

Zul.—Oh, delightful!   Let me see.

Ay.—And me!

[*They take the glass and look at themselves in
it—then turn away disappointed.*

Ay.—Why, we can't see ourselves in it!

Fat.—No—it's a fairy looking-glass.

Zul.—What's the good of that?

Fat.—Nobody can see anything in it but me.

Ay.—What a shame!

Fat.—And I can't see anything in it but the
Beast.

Zul. and Ay.—Oh, how horrid!

Fat.—By looking in this glass I can always see if he is well, when I am away from him. [*Starts.*] Oh, look—he is ill—he is dying—he is lying on the ground in the garden—I must go to him—quick—quick!   [*Runs out.*

Zul.—Father, I should like to go too.

Ab. C.—Go too? nonsense, you're not wanted—mustn't go to places without being asked!

Ay.—Oh, do let us go—it would be such fun.

Zul.—Besides, perhaps the Beast is dead by this time, and then he won't mind.

Ab. C.—Well, well, we'll see when I've finished my pipe—you must leave me in peace till then.

Ay—Come along, then, Zuleika, we'll go and put on our things.

Zul.—Oh, what fun it will be!   [*Exeunt Zul. and Ay.*

Curtain.

Scene *VI.*—*The Prince's garden.*

Fat.—Where are you, my dear Beast? [*Starts.*]   Oh, there you are!   [*Kneels by him.*] Alas! I fear you are dead—I have killed you. Beast—wake up—I am here—it is Beauty come back to you! Dear Beast I wish you would get

up—I like you so much now—I'm very sorry I
didn't say I loved you—I do really—I love you
very much!   [*The Beast springs up—his fur
falls off.*

Pr.—Beauty, my love! you have turned me
into a prince again!

Fat.—What! are you the same who was a
beast?

Pr.—Of course I am—and now I am never
going to be a beast any more, but a beautiful
young prince.

Fat.— Oh, how nice!

Pr.—And if you will marry me, you shall be a
beautiful young princess!

Fat.—That's nicer still! Of course I will,
then!

Duet.   Air—'Là ci darem.'

Pr.—Then I will be your husband,
    And you shall be my wife;
We will love each other, and lead a happy
    life.

Enter Zul. and Ay., followed by Ab. C.

Zul.—Why, what's all this about?

Ay.—Who is this young man?

Pr.—I'm Prince Furryskin, at your service.

Fat.—And I'm gong to be the Princess Furryskin.

Zul (to Fat).—Then why did you say he was a beast?

Ay.—What horrid stories you told us!

Fat.—I didn't tell stories—he was a beast—wasn't he, papa?

Ab. C.—He certainly was the last time I saw him—a regular beast, I'll answer for that.

Pr.—Dear ladies, don't be angry—I will tell you how it was—a wicked fairy turned me into a beast, and said I shouldn't turn back into a prince again till a beautiful girl said she loved me.

Fat.—And so when I said I loved him, he jumped up and turned into a prince.

Pr.—And now you have all come, I hope you will stay to dinner. (*Calls*) Here, Molinko! where's the lazy beggar now- here Molinko!

Enter Molinko.

Mol.—Yes!

Pr.—Is dinner ready?

Mol.—No!

Pr.—We shall be six to dinner—can you manage that?

Mol.—No!

Fat.—Oh, yes you can, dear Molinko—and we'll help you to get it ready—may we?

Mol.—Yes.

Pr.—And then we'll be married.

Fat.—And I shall be a princess.

Zul. and Ay.—And we will be the bridesmaids.

Ab. C.—And I will be the father-in-law.

Mol.—And I'll eat the wedding cake.

Finale. Tune—'The Young Recruit.'

And we'll be a merry party
  On this happy wedding day *(bis)*.
We will all be gay and hearty
  As we dance and sing and play.
    Tra la la la la, &c.
      Curtain.

King Alfred and the Cakes

DRAMATIS PERSONÆ

ALFRED, King of England.
EARL ETHELRED.
A Minstrel.
THE NEATHERD'S WIFE.

KING ALFRED AND THE CAKES.

Scene—The inside of the Neatherd's hut in the Island of Athelney. Door *Left* corner. The rough walls are hung round with mugs, platters, pots, pans: the floor is strewn with straw; to the *Right* a rough wooden table littered with kitchen things; to the *Left,* a charcoal fire built roughly round with stones: a wooden stool near the fire, another by the table. When the curtain rises King Alfred is discovered sitting on stool, to *Left* by the fire. He is dressed is an old tattered brown doublet edged with fur, sandals on his feet, and instead of stockings he wears leather straps bound round, from ankle to knee. His hair is long, reaching to shoulders: his beard rough and uncombed. The Good-wife stands at the table busily mixing some dough in a wooden bowl. She wears a coarse apron over very coarse clothes; her head is covered with a shawl, her sleeves are pushed up as far as they will go.

The Good-Wife (turning the dough on to the table and kneading it.)—Now if you would eat well to-night, stranger, you had best leave off

dreaming there by there and attend to me.
These are rye-cakes for the supper. Do you
hear? And they must be watched while they are
baking . . . (*repeating slowly and solemnly*)
watched while they are baking—(*sharply*) do
you hear me?

King Alfred (dreamily)—Yes, my good dame
. . . washed while they are baking . . . .

Good-Wife (turning round hands on hips, and
looking at him)—Washed! Watched, I said: I
declare the fellow's half asleep! Wake up, my
man, and listen to me! (*kneading dough again.*)
They must be watched well, for they are quick
to burn . . . (*dividing the dough into four
parts and making it into round cakes*) and what's
more, you shall be the one to watch them for me.

King Alfred (still dreamily)—I . . . ?

Good-Wife—Yes, you . . . you might as
well do that as sit dreaming over the fire all day.
I have enough to do as it is: there are the pigs
and the hens to feed, the beasts to see to, and a-
many more things besides. I cannot spare the
time, although I am loath to leave my fine cakes
with such a lazy fellow.

King Alfred—I will watch them carefully for
you, good dame.

"They must be watched while they are baking,"—Page 88

Good-Wife (going to fire and puting the cake carefully on the top)—So be it.   Now, look you, they must be brown and yet not too brown, and when one side is nicely done you must turn them, but carefully.   So—(*showing him*).

King Alfred—Yes . . . yes . . . it shall be done, never fear.

Good-Wife—But mind this, my man, they will burn if you do not take care, for the charcoal is hot.   You must never take your eyes off them a moment—never a moment, do you hear?   or you will go hungry this night to bed, and to-morrow and the next day.   We cannot afford to waste good food in this lonely place.

King Alfred (half to himself)—Ay, it is a lonely place, and savage enough and safe enough even for me.

Good-Wife (going to the door, *Left* corner)— Look to your work now, or it will be the worse for us all.   (*exit.*)

Alfred (resting his head on his hand, and speaking slowly, as if thinking aloud)—Ay, my good dame, there you spoke true.   I have more work to do than you think, and if it be not well done it will indeed be worse for us all.   O England! . . . O my country!   O my poor peo-

ple, down-trodden by the bitter, treacherous
Danes, what can I, thy King, do to save thee?
Here in hiding—alone—with my brave soldiers
scattered—defeated—slain . . . what can I
do for thee, O my country? (*rising.*) While
there is life in me, and a brain to think and a
heart to beat for thee, I will never give in . . .
the tide *must* turn. . . . There is a Power
above that will never desert the righteous. . .
Courage . . . Courage . . . We shall
conquer these foes that come only to steal our
gold and our lands, our lives and our peace.
England shall be freed from these robbers. (*sits
down.*) . . . Oh, if ever I win back my crown
and kingdom, I solemnly vow that the third part
of my time I will give up to deeds of charity—
the third part of my gold shall be given to the
poor—the . . .

Good-wife (entering angrily, and rushing to
the fire)—They are burnt . . . they are black
. . . I smelt them burning half way down
the path. Shame . . . shame on you
stranger! O the fool that I was to leave them
with you! . . . O fool, fool that you were to
let them burn! Look at them . . . Look at
them . . . (*shaking one in his face.*)   Good-

for-nothing, you would rather starve than work
. . . you would see good food burn and never
trouble to lift a finger to save it . . . a pretty
fellow, i' faith! (*a knock is heard at the door.*)

King Alfred—What was that?

Good-Wife (angrier than ever)— . . . A
pretty fellow! You have eaten my food and
slept under my roof for six weeks, and what do
you give me in return? You burn my cakes,
my good rye-cakes, till they are fit for nothing
but to throw to the pigs! Oh! (Slaps him on
the cheek: enter *Earl Ethelred* followed by Minstrel.) Out of this house you go this very moment! . . . I will have no more to do with
you and your lazy, wasteful ways . . .

Alfred (interrupting)—Ah! At last! My
friend, my friend, what news?

Ethelred—Good news, my Lord!

Good-Wife (open-mouthed)—My Lord!
What next, I wonder!

The Minstrel (kneeling and kissing the *King's*
hand)—Ah! your Majesty! How good it is to
find you safe and well!

Good-Wife—Your Majesty! The man's
mad!

King Alfred—The news! I pray you, if you
love me, speak! I know nothing!

Ethelred—Hubba the Dane is dead!

King Alfred—God be praised!

The Minstrel—Their Raven Standard is taken. We have it.

Ethelred—Hubba grew too bold. Wales he invaded, leaving every town in flames: then came he to Devon, and there he met his fate at Kenworth Castle.

The Minstrel—The Devon men were few but desperate, they determined to conquer or to die . . . .

King Alfred (impatiently)—Yes, yes!

Ethelred—By night they rushed on the enemy, and took them unawares. Hubba was slain, the Standard taken, and their whole army fled in breathless fear. . . .

The Minstrel (triumphantly)—'Tis said their Raven Standard brings them fortune; now they have lost it, now the tide is turned. I will make a song of it, O King! . . .

Good-Wife (very much frightened)—King!

The Minstrel—And I will sing it to thee, King, on the day when thou shalt come again to thy throne.

KingAlfred—Ay, the tide is turned. . . . I feel it . . . we shall conquer now. Do you, each of you, take a different path over the country and spread the news far and wide. Bid all who love England and King Alfred come swiftly and well armed to Selwood Forest.

Good-Wife—King Alfred! Burned my cakes black as cinders . . . oh, mercy . . . mercy . . . and I boxed his ears for it! . . Woe's me! . . . woe's me! . . .

King Alfred (smiling)—This good soul hath sheltered me right nobly all these weary weeks.

Good-Wife—(falling on her knees)—Mercy, mercy, Sir King!

King Alfred—'Tis I who cry to you for mercy, my good dame. I burnt your cakes; but have no fear, ye shall have a gold piece for every one, and my hearty thanks for all your kindness. (*raising her to her feet.*) I fear my dreamy ways were not much to your liking. But come, my friends, let us go, and speedily. There is no time to be lost; (*going to door*) we have each our work to do.

Ethelred and *Minstrel* (following)—Ay, forward! Forward!

King Alfred—To Victory! (*exit all save* Good-Wife.)

Good-Wife (at the door, watching them out of sight)—To think of it . . . to think of it

. . . (*going to table.*)   And I never knew
. . . I never guessed . . . (*taking up a cake.*)   Ay, black as a cinder . . . to think
of it, and I slapped him with these very fingers
. . . (*in a whisper.*)   Him! The King
. . . our good King Alfred. (*loudly.*)
God save him! . . . God give him victory
over his enemies!

CURTAIN

Jack and the Beanstalk

DRAMATIS PERSONÆ

MRS. BROWN.
JACK (her son).
COUNTRYMAN.
OGRE.
GRUMPS (his wife.)

JACK AND THE BEANSTALK.

A Play in Three Acts.

ACT I.

Mrs. Brown (spinning)—Seven o'clock—It's time for supper! but there's nothing to eat in the house—what I shall say to Jack when he comes in I don't know. And I know the first thing he'll say will be, 'Well, mother! what is there for supper?' Ah, there he is outside. [*Jack heard whistling and singing.*] He is a nice boy certainly, and a very good boy too sometimes, but he is a very noisy one.

Enter Jack.

Jack—Mother, what is there for supper?

Mrs. Brown—There, I knew it! Don't shout, Jack, I'm not deaf.

Jack—All right, I won't. (*Whispering*) Mother, what is there for supper?

Mrs. Brown—I never saw such a boy! He thinks of nothing but his meals!

Jack—Of course I do, at meal times. That's right and proper! (*sings*).

Yes, yes, my appetite
Is always good for meals at night—
You mustn't starve me quite,
You'll see me grow quite thin and white.

Mrs. Brown—Well, well, I can't help that,
I'd rather see you pink and fat—
I don't know what to be at,
I feel inclined to stew the cat.

Jack—Now then, let's lay the cloth.

Mrs. Brown—You may lay the cloth on the table if you like, but there's nothing else to put on it.

Jack—Nothing for supper!

Mrs. Brown—Not one crumb.

Jack—Let's buy something then.

Mrs. Brown—We haven't any money to buy anything with.

Jack—Let's sell something.

Mrs. Brown—We've got nothing to sell.

Jack (making a dart at the cat).—Let's sell the cat!

Mrs. Brown—Sell the cat! What would you get by that?

Jack—We should get scratches, spits, and mews, I should think. Ha, ha!

Mrs. Brown—Ah! It's nothing to laugh at!

there is only one thing we can sell, and that is the cow.

Jack—What, mother, sell our pretty Brindle?

Mrs. Brown—Alas, yes! We must part with her, there is nothing else to be done.

Jack—How much will you get for her?

Mrs. Brown—Well, neighbor Hodge would give me fifteen pounds for her.

Jack—Fifteen pounds! Dear me, how many breakfasts, dinners, and suppers I could have for that.

Mrs. Brown (going out)—Oh that I should have such a greedy, greedy boy as this! Now take care of the house, and don't you get into mischief for once.

Jack—All right, mother, I'll take care of it.

[*Exit Mrs. Brown.*

Jack—There! Now I'm the master of the house! Now, what shall I do next? If I could find the cat I would tie him up in the pudding bag. Perhaps I had better learn my spelling for to-morrow.

[*He takes book and plays at football with it.*

Enter Countryman.

Countryman—Good evening, young man.

Jack—Good evening, old man.

Countryman—You're not very polite.

Jack—I'm not generally considered so .

Countryman—Where's the master of the house?

Jack—Here.   I'm the master of the house.

Countryman—What, do you live alone here?

Jack—Yes, except my mother—she lives with me, but that doesn't count.

Countryman—Where is your mother gone to?

Jack—She has gone to see neighbor Hodge about selling the cow.

Countryman—Selling the cow?

Jack—Yes.   We're very poor.   We haven't got anything to eat in the house.

Countryman—Nothing to eat! that's bad. How much will she sell it for?

Jack—Oh, I don't know.   As much as she can get.

Countryman—Pity she did'nt sell her to me, I want a cow myself.

Jack—Do you?   Look here, what fun it would be to sell you the cow before mother comes back! it would be a surprise.

Countryman—Not a bad idea.   (Aside) I will deceive this innocent child, and buy his cow for nothing.

Jack—What will you give me for it?   You

must give a great deal, you know. Let me see, more than fifteen pounds, I should think.

Countryman—I don't know that I can give you that much in ordinary money, but I have something of much more value in my pocket.

[*Produces beans.*

Jack—Oh, what lovely things!

Countryman—I should think so! it is not often you come across anything like that.

Jack—Then how many of those will you give me for the cow?

Countryman—Well, let me see—you say you want fifteen pounds for the cow, and these are much more valuable. I will give you a dozen.

Jack—A dozen, all right. (Aside) That's a splendid bargain! I hope I am not taking the poor man in.

Countryman—All right, that's a bargain. Where is the beast?

Jack—There she is, outside—go out of doors and turn down the path, it is the first cow to the left.

Countryman—Your hand on it.

Jack (sings)—Then there's my hand—
    I understand!

Countryman—To fortune 'tis the way—

You ne'er again
Will have, 'tis plain,
The chance you've had to-day!

        [Repeat together and dance.
[Mrs. Brown comes in and sees the others danc-
ing.

Mrs. Brown—I hope I'm not interrupting you.

Countryman (still dancing)—Not in the least
ma'am, not in the least, thank you—I happened
to be calling, ma'am, and as you were not in I
thought I would dance a little to pass the time
until your return.

Mrs. Brown—Thank you, that is very kind of
you, but I am sorry to say that I have not the
pleasure of your acquaintance.

Countryman—No, ma'am, no, ma'am, that is
quite true, that is why I began to think it was
time you should.

Mrs. Brown (aside)—He is too polite for my
taste—I never trust people who are polite.

Countryman—In the meantime your son has
been entertaining me—what a charming, well-
bred young gentleman he is!

Mrs. Brown—It is not often he has that said
of him.

Countryman—He is just the young gentleman I like.

[*Holds his hand to Jack—they dance together on tiptoe, Mrs. Brown following angrily after them—Countryman dances out.*

Mrs. Brown—I never saw such doings as this! as if we had nothing better to do! sit down and get your spelling book, and see if you can keep quiet for five minutes.

[*Jack sits down with his book.*

Jack—C O W—What does C O W spell, mother?

Mrs. Brown—C O W spells Cow.

Jack (smiling to himself)—Cow! I thought it did!

Mrs. Brown—Neighbor Hodge says he will buy Brindle—I wonder where she is, I must go out and see her.

Jack—Oh no, you need not, I have just seen her.

Mrs. Brown—(looking out of the window)—I don't see her anywhere! where can she be?

Jack—Perhaps she is sitting under a cabbage leaf, or she's climbed the cherry tree—oh no, I forgot, she is a grizzly cow and can't climb trees.

Mrs. Brown—Hold your tongue, you naughty boy! go and see where she is.

Jack—I know where she is without going to

see—at least I know where she is not, and that's in the garden.

Mrs. Brown—Not in the garden! Where is she then?

Jack—I've sold her.

Mrs. Brown—You've sold her! You naughty, bad boy!

Jack—Not at all, I've saved you the trouble.

Mrs. Brown—What did you get for her?

Jack—Ah, mother, you will be pleased!

Mrs. Brown—What, have you got more than twenty pounds?—you are a good boy!

Jack—Well, not for more than fifteen in money. Look—— [*He puts his hands into his pockets.*

Mrs. Brown—Be quick! I'm dying to know what you got. [*Jack pulls out a handful of beans.*

Mrs. Brown (impatiently)—Come, never mind those stupid things—give me the money!

[*Takes the handful and throws them out of the window.*

Jack—Stop, stop, mother that's the money! You are throwing away the money that I got for the cow.

Mrs. Brown—What! Do you mean to say that you sold my cow for a few worthless beans? you wretched boy, you have ruined me! you have ruined your mother!

Jack—But, mother, Mr. Barleycorn said they were worth a great deal more! a great, great deal more!

Mrs. Brown—But, he did not speak the truth —you stupid boy.

Jack—I thought grown-up people always spoke the truth.

Mrs. Brown—Well, you'll know better after this, I hope. You stupid, stupid boy! Whatever are we to do?

Jack—Well, I do think it is a pity my beautiful beans were thrown away. [*Goes to window to look.*] Why, what's that in the garden? Look, mother, look!

Mrs. Brown (rushing)—Is it Brindle? Brindle come back?

Jack—No, no something far better than that —it is something growing, growing right up to the sky.

Mrs. Brown—I do believe it's a beanstalk!

Jack—A beanstalk? Yes, it is my beans growing! Oh, mother, how exciting! I'll climb up and see where it goes to.

Mrs. Brown—No, no, don't go up into the

sky in that way without knowing where you are
going.

Jack—I must, mother, I must! Good-bye!
I'll bring you back something beautiful from
the clouds—perhaps another cow as good as
Brindle.

[*He climbs on to window sill and sings.*

Song.

Up, upon a beanstalk, high as a balloon,
All among the little clouds, a-sailing round the
    moon.

Mrs. Brown—Oh, if you are going, mind you
        come back soon—

I don't like your climbing things that lead up
    to the moon!

Curtain.

ACT II.

SCENE 1—*Interior of the Ogre's castle. A
large kitchen.*

Enter Jack, cautiously, looking round.

Jack—Oh! at last! What a long beanstalk!
I thought I should never get to the top. And
now that I am here, I wonder where I am! It

looked like a castle from outside.   Ah! here is some one coming.

Enter Grumps, the Ogre's wife.

Grumps—Shsh! Shoo!! Go away!!! [*Waving frying-pan at Jack.*]   No boys here.

Jack—But, my good soul——

Grumps—No, I ain't your good soul. Go away, I tell you.

Jack—But why?

Grumps—Because this is the Ogre's castle, and he will be back directly for his dinner.

Jack—And what will he have for his dinner?

Grumps—You, if you stay any longer!   So I advise you to disappear.

Jack—That's all very well, but where am I to go to?

Grumps—Go back to the place you came from.

Jack—But I don't know the way.

Grumps—How did you get here, then?

Jack—I happened to meet a fairy after I left the beanstalk, and she directed me to your house.

Grumps—Well, happen to meet another then, and let her direct you back.   If you wait much longer you'll meet the Ogre, and then you won't need any directions.

[*Ogre heard outside.*

Ogre.   Fee, fi, fo, fum!

I smell the blood of an Englishman.

Be he alive, or be he dead,

I'll grind his bones to make my bread.

Jack—What is that?

Grumps—The Ogre—the Ogre!

Jack—Oh! do hide me somewhere—please!

Grumps (opening oven door).—Quick, then! Here you are.   Jump in here!

[*Jack jumps in.   Grumps closes door just, as Ogre comes in.*

Ogre (sings).—Fee, fi, fo, fum!

I smell the blood of an Englishman.

What have you got for my dinner to-day, you useless woman?   What is there? come, tell me quick!

Grumps—A nice little kid that I caught on the mountain.

Ogre—I don't believe it!   There is something else!

[*Sniffing.*]—What is that I smell?   It's a boy —I'm sure it's a boy!   [*Jumps up.*

Grumps—A boy—nonsense!   Where should a boy come from?   [*Stands in front of oven.*

Ogre—I'm sure there's a boy in that oven— and what is more, I mean to look. [*Goes to oven.*

Grumps (in front of the oven)—Very well—

if you open the oven now, your dinner will be spoiled, that's all—the kid won't be done enough.

Ogre—Hum, ha—well—I won't look in it till after dinner then—but mind the kid is done right, or I'll throw you out of the window. I'm going to change my seven-leagued boots, and when I come back it must be ready.

[*Exit, singing 'Fee' fi, fo, fum.'*

Grumps (to Jack)—Quick, quick! now is your time! [*Jack comes out.*] I don't think it would be safe for you to try to escape now, as he might see you from the window—but he always goes to sleep after his dinner—when you hear him snore go gently out. [*Puts him behind a chest.*

Enter Ogre, singing, 'Fee, fi, fo, fum,' &c. Sits down, ties a napkin round his neck.

Ogre—Well, where's that kid? Isn't it ready?

Grumps—Coming—coming—here it is! it's no good my putting it on the table to get cold while you're half a mile off, is it?

Ogre—Silence, you horrid old woman! or I'll eat you for my pudding. [*He dines: she waits on him. Song ad lib.*] Now then clear away, old witch—and bring me my fairy hen!

[*Grumps goes to where Jack is hiding and gets*

the hen—he puts his head out, Grumps pushes him down again.

Ogre—Now then, is that hen coming? I never saw such a house—the hens are always late!

[*Sings.*

Come, make haste—make no delaying!
Do you hear what I am saying?
If that hen has not been laying
You shall die this very day!

Grumps (bring hen).—Here she is, your call
    obeying—
Here's the pretty beast displaying
All her talents, ever laying
Fifteen golden eggs a day.

[*Repeat together.*

Ogre—Now then, what are you standing there singing for? Go and get my money bag ready —and my fairy fiddle—all the things I shall want [*Grumps going, Ogre calls after her*]. And Hi! [*She turns back.*] If I should happen to go to sleep presently——

Grumps—Happen! Why, you never do anything else!

Ogre—Hold your tongue, you monster—or I will put you into the oven! I was going to say— I wish you to sit on the door mat, in case anyone should disturb me if I should happen to go to sleep.

Grumps—All right. Now you have everything comfortable. Your hen and money bag—and your armchair.

Ogre—I thought I heard something behind that chest! the dog isn't here, is he? I won't have him left in the room.

Grumps—No, no. He isn't there.

Ogre—How do you know? Go and look.

Grumps (takes stick and pokes behind chest where Jack is)—Sh—sh!

Ogre (imitating her)—Sh! indeed! What's the use of that? Here, give it to me, I'll soon see if the creature is there. [*Runs at one side of chest and bangs stick down, Jack runs out at the other—and the same at the other side.*] There, that's the way to do things! there doesn't seem to be anything there. You were right for once—so you may go and leave me in peace. [*Exit Grumps singing. Ogre strokes hen.*] Pretty creature! And you are not only pretty—you are clever—that's better still! and not only clever, you are good, which is best of all! for you know how to lay me fifteen golden eggs every day. Come, where are they? [*Lifts her up and finds the eggs.*] Ah— that will do for my pocket money till to-morrow—so now you may just wait there until this evening. [*Goes to sleep. Soft music. Jack comes out softly—carries the hen behind the chest, and as he does so falls over something with a crash. Ogre wakes, looks round.*] Why, what was that? I'm sure I heard a noise— it must have been a cinder falling out of the fire —or I woke myself by snoring—though I don't believe I do snore, though that old Grumps always declares I do. How tiresome to be awake, just when I was so comfortable! However, I'll count my money now and go to sleep again afterwards.

      [*Draws the money bag forwards. Sings.*

Gold! gold! gold! gold!
Bright and yellow, hard and cold.
Pounds and shillings, pennies too.
All for me, and none for you.

There don't seem to be as many as there were last time. I believe Grumps has been taking some I'll hang her up to the top of the castle presently, if I remember it. [*Makes a knot in nightcap.*] There, that will remind me. [*Ties up bag.*] There—there are a great many starving people in the world who would be glad to have only a little of what that bag contains—Ha, ha!

they shan't have any of it—I'll keep it all for myself—every bit! *Puts money bag behind his
chair, where it rolls down.*] Now I'll see if I
can't go to sleep again. [*Music as before.
Ogre snores. Jack comes out, and tries to draw
money bag—it is too heavy—at last he succeeds,
but rolls over with it. Ogre starts up. Jack lies
down behind the bag.*] Why, it's that stupid
money bag that has rolled over—stupid of me not
to put it up safely! [*Going to sleep—Jack
creeps out—Ogre starts up again—Jack goes
back.*] It's no use—I can't do it! I'll make
Mrs. Grumps come and play me to sleep. Here
—Grumps! Come! [*Enter Grumps.*] Why
don't you come more quickly? Where are you?

Grumps—I was on the door mat, of course.

Ogre—It's very kind of me to let you sit there
—very kind, do you hear?

Grumps—I hear—yes.

Ogre—Then don't presume to answer. Take
my fairy violin and play me to sleep, and mind
you don't make any of those squeaks, or I'll
wring your neck.

[*Grumps plays. . .The Ogre hums the tune she
is playing, and gradually goes off. She lays
down the violin and makes a sign to Jack, he
comes out quietly.*

Grumps (whispering)—Follow me quietly, and I will go on and open the doors.

[*Takes big keys off Ogre's lap and exit.*

Jack (aside)—Yes—but I'll take a few of these things with me! [*Pushes the money bag out of the window—takes the hen under one arm and the violin under the other.*] Now I'll make a rush past her and get down the beanstalk and take these home to my mother.

[*Violin heard squeaking and calling 'Master! master!' louder and louder.*]

Enter Grumps.

Grumps—Where is he? Quick, quick, you will have time to get away before he wakes. Why, where is he? Alas! alas! he is gone— the ungrateful little wretch—and he has taken everything with him. Oh, what shall I do?

[*Violin heard calling. Ogre wakes.*

Ogre—What, why are all the noises in Christendom turned loose here to-day? What is all this? [*Wakes quite up, and sees Grumps. She rushes out with a shriek.*] What is all this? [*Puts his cap straight.*]—Ha, what is this knot Ha—I remember, Grumps!

[*Dashes out singing, "Fee, fi, fo fum!"*

Curtain.

ACT III.

SCENE—*Mrs. Brown's house. Mrs. Brown and Jack beautifully dressed.*

Jack—How comfortable we are, mother!

Mrs. Brown—Yes, and what beautiful clothes we have on!

Jack—It seems a great deal more than a week since I sold the cow, doesn't it?

Mrs. Brown—Yes, indeed it does. I was quite in despair that day, till I saw you coming back again with the fairy hen, the money bag and the violin.

Jack—And ever since we have had everything we can wish for, and we have been able to feed all the poor people in the village besides.

Mrs. Brown—That reminds me—I said I would go out to see neighbor Hodge—but it is too muddy to walk, so I have ordered the carriage.

Jack—Which one? The open one drawn by six cream-colored horses?

Mrs. Brown—No—I think it is too cold for that—I shall go in the shut glass coach, drawn by eight piebalds. I am so accustomed to driving now!

Jack—You see how right I was to climb up to

the Ogre's castle and get all these things for you!
But, mother, I do wonder what he has done without them!   Don't you sometimes wonder how it
is he has never come to look for them?

Mrs. Brown—Oh—what a terrible idea!   Suppose he were to come!

Jack—I never thought of that—I almost think
it would be safest to cut the beanstalk down, as
then there will be no way for him to come.

Mrs. Brown—I think it would—but what a
pity it seems—that dear beanstalk, to which we
owe so much!   [*Gets up and looks out of window
at it.   She starts back.*]   Jack!   Jack!   It is too
late!   See—see—there is some one coming down
from the sky—a gigantic form—it must be the
Ogre!

Jack—It is—it is the Ogre!   Where is my
hatchet? Quick!   [*Seizes hatchet and rushes out.*]

Mrs. Brown—Stay—stay!   Jack!   Here!   Oh!
[*Then watching from window*].   The Ogre has
reached the ground—he has drawn his sword—
Jack has attacked him!   The Ogre has struck at
him, Jack has jumped aside—he has cut off the
Ogre's legs with his axe—the Ogre falls—Jack
has cut off his head!   Ah—my brave boy!

Enter Jack with the Ogre's head.

Jack—There, mother—there is the monster's head, he will never trouble us any more—and as for poor Grumps, his companion, I believe he killed the day I left the castle. So now we can be happy for the rest of our days.

[*They dance round it. As they leave off a knock is heard at the door.*]

Mrs. Brown—Oh—who can that be—not another Ogre?

Jack—No, I don't think that is very likely! Besides, he'll soon go away when he sees that! [*Pointing to head.*] Come in!

Enter Countryman, much better dressed.

Jack—Mr. Barleycorn!

Countryman—That is my name certainly, but I think I must have made a mistake. [*Looking round.*] This is not the house that stood here before, surely?

Mrs. Brown—Yes, it is only rather differently furnished!

Countryman (sees head and starts)—That ornament is new, certainly, since I was here. Then you are the lady who wouldn't dance with me?

Mrs. Brown—And you are the gentleman who bought my poor Brindle for some beans?

Countryman—Exactly—I am, and a very

good cow she was.   I came to know if you could sell me another like her.

Mrs. Brown—Well, I must say I wonder you dare show your face here again after deceiving my innocent boy in the way you did about those beans!

Jack—Come, come, mother, after all you need not complain of the beans, for they have been the cause of all our good luck.

Mrs. Brown—It is quite true.   (To Country-man)—I forgive you, and I hope you have taken good care of my pretty Brindle.

Countryman—Indeed   I   have.   She   has brought me good luck, too—ever since I had her I have been growing richer and richer.

Jack—Then, you see, our bargain was a good one after all!   For if it had not been for you I should never have climbed up the beanstalk.

> Then there's my hand,
> My trusty friend,
> To fortune 'twas the way!
> We ne'er again
> Shall have, 'tis plain,
> The chance we had that day!
>   [*Repeat together and dance.*
>
>   *Curtain.*

Little Bo-Peep

LITTLE BO-PEEP.

F. H. S.

This stage play requires an even number of girls—three to six couples from four to seven years of age.

The girls dress in Shepherdess costume—short kilt skirts, looped overskirts of flowered goods, laced girdles and puff waists, black hose, slippers with high heels and big ribbon bows, and large brimmed straw hats. Each one carries a crook—a cane or parasol handle, with several gaily-colored ribbon streamers attached to the handle.

An essential part of this drill is the flock of "lost sheep," which consists of seven boys who can bleat well. They are hidden at the following places behind the scenes; right front, left front, center right, center left, rear right, rear left, center rear. They perform as indicated.

Prelude: Before the curtain rises a chorus of children come before it and sing the story of "Bo-Peep and her sheep:

2.   Little Bo-Peep fell fast asleep
And dreamt she heard them bleating, bleating,
But when she awoke she found it a joke
For still they were all fleeting, fleeting,
But when she awoke she found it a joke
For still they were all fleeting.

3.   Then up she took her little crook,
Determined for to find them
She found them indeed, but it made her heart
    bleed,
For they'd left their tails behind them, behind
    them.
She found (etc.).

Song: Bo-Peep and Her Sheep.

4.   It happened one day Bo-Peep did stray
Along a meadow hard by, hard by,
There she espied the tails side by side
All hung on a tree to dry, to dry.
There she espied (etc.).

5.   She heaved a sigh and wiped her eye
And ran o'er hill and dale, Oh! dale Oh!
And tried what she could, as a shepherdess
    should,
To tack to each sheep its own tail, Oh! tail Oh!
And tried (etc.).

Part I: "Bo-Peep"

(A) Pianist strikes chord, curtain rises. Girls enter in two lines, one from right front, one from left front. They keep time with their crooks and march diagonally across the stage, leaders meeting at center rear, lines thence forming diagonally across stage thus:

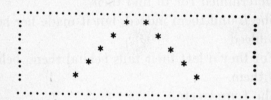

(B) They hold crooks horizontally toward each other, then up, then together again, then at sides.

(C) Girls shade eyes with hands and lean toward outside of stage, as tho' looking for the sheep.

(D) Lean toward center of stage.

(E) Girls put hands to ears and lean outside as tho' listening for sheep.

(F) Lean toward center and listen.

(G) Partners shake crooks sadly at each other, in time to music.

(H) Repeat (C).

(I)   Repeat (E).

(J)   Each girl pretends to yawn by holding hand over mouth and very, very, slowly raising head.

(K)   Slowly rub right eye with fist, then left eye, then alternate.

(L)   Slowly stretch right arm, then left arm, alternately.

(M)   Shut eyes and move head slowly from shoulder to shoulder, letting it fall with a sleepy jerk.   Drop crooks.

(N)   Clasp hands, put them under right cheek, and slowly bring head over on right shoulder, yet with a little jerk at the last.   Head remains on shoulder during several counts.   Then hands are put under the left cheek and head is nodded to left side.

(O)   They slowly settle down to floor in different sleeping positions.   Some have both hands under their cheek, some have hands over head, etc.   All close their eyes.

Part II: "The Sheep"

(1)   While girls retain position as in (O) a far-away bleat is heard at center rear (the "sheep" putting his hand over his mouth to give

it a vibratory, distant sound). Girls start up quickly, raise crooks, as though saying "Hark!" and turning they look toward center rear.

(2) A far-away bleat is heard at right front, girls turn quickly and lean forward in that direction with hands to ears.

(3) A far-away bleat is heard at left front and girls turn quickly and gaze in that direction, hands shading eyes.

(4) A muffled bleat is heard at rear and girls turn quickly, raising crooks toward each other.

(5) A muffled bleat is heard at center right and girls turn in that direction, rising on tiptoe to listen.

(6) Muffled bleat is heard at center left and girls turn and gaze in that direction.

(7) Louder bleat is heard at right front, and the line at right side follows leader off quickly in that direction, other line gazing after.

(8) As last girl disappears in (7) a bleat is heard at left front and the line of girls march off briskly in that direction.

(9) Loud bleat heard at left rear, and the line of girls enters from right front and skips diagonally across and off at left rear.

(10) Loud bleat heard at right rear and line

of girls enters from left front and skips diagonally across and off at right rear.

(11) Loud bleats heard from both center left and center right. The two lines enter in double column at center rear and skip off at center left and center right, waving crooks gaily.

(12) Loud bleat heard at center rear and two lines of girls rush in from right and left front, race diagonally off at center rear.

(13) Loud bleats heard from all sides, girls rush in in a double column from center rear, and run off at different parts of the stage.

Part III: "The Tails"

After a considerable pause the girls enter walking slowly. Each one holds a twig with seven or eight tails (twists of cotton) hanging therefrom. They shake their heads sadly, wipe an eye and look at the tails. The bleats then break out on all sides and girls run off with the tails.

(Curtain.)

The Princess and the Swineherd

DRAMATIS PERSONÆ

The Emperor.
The Princess.
Her Maids of Honor.
The Swineherd, who is really The Prince.
Attendants.

He doesn't wear a crown. (Do put yours straight, papa).—Page 131

THE PRINCESS AND THE SWINE-HERD.

The Emperor's Palace.

SCENE—The hall in the palace. Very little furniture; chairs, scattered untidily, here and there, one of them overturned; the rug or carpet is rumpled up. Entrances, *Left* and *Right* near back of stage. When the curtain rises the Princess is discovered playing at ball with four or five Maids of Honor. Princess to *Left* at front of the stage; Maids placed at intervals round the room. They throw a golden ball from one to the other. The Princess throws; Third Maid of Honor misses the catch.

The Princess—Oh, you stupid, stupid thing! That is the third time you have missed your throw.

Third Maid (muttering)—It wasn't straight.

The Princess (sharply)—What did you say? Of course it was straight; Princesses always throw straight. (*To the others*) Don't they?

The Others—Oh yes! Yes! (*To the Third Maid*) How can you say such things?

The Princess—Now don't stand chattering there; begin again, and remember, after this, the first who misses shan't play any more. (*They throw again; the Princess misses.*)

The Princess (angrily)—There! That was your fault; you can't throw straight any of you, and after all, it's a very silly game. (*Enter Emperor, Right entrance. He wears a long embroidered dressing-gown, bedroom slippers down at the heel, and a golden crown, which being a little too big, slips down over one ear.*)

Emperor (fussily)—What is all this about? Dear, dear! Playing at ball again, are you? And what a mess you have made! Look at those chairs . . . and the rug . . . and your hair . . . My dear daughter, you are not fit to be seen; go and tidy yourself directly; there is a handsome young Prince coming to see you. (*The Maids of Honor bustle about putting things straight.*)

The Princess (carelessly tossing the ball and catching it again)—A Prince? Who is he, and what is he coming to see me for?

The Emperor—He lives in the next kingdom, and he is coming to ask you to marry him.

The Princess—Why! That Prince? I shall

certainly not marry *him,* and if he comes I shan't see him.

Emperor (crossly)—You are a naughty, tiresome girl, and it's time you were married. I am tired of your tantrums and hoity-toity ways. This is the sixth prince you have sent away.

The Princess—We'll they were none of them good enough; one had too big a nose, and another couldn't speak without gobbling like a turkey, and the rest were as stupid as owls, but this one is the worst of all.

The Emperor—He is very handsome, my love.

The Princess (tossing her head)—I don't care! His kingdom is such a little one, and his palace isn't a palace at all, only a plain, ordinary castle with not more than a hundred servants in it, and he doesn't wear a crown. (Do put yours straight Papa.) Besides, I don't want to get married.

The Emperor (a little angrily)—But *I* wish you to . . .

The Princess (stamping her foot)—And I don't wish to.

The Emperor (with a big sigh)—Oh dear! Oh dear! What would the poor dear Empress say if she were alive! (*A knock at the door.*

Enter by Left, two servants with a silver casket or box.)

The Emperor (rubbing his hands joyfully) — Now we shall see if this won't make you change your mind. This is a present for you, from the young Prince, my love.

The Princess (clapping her hands)—A present! Oh, if it should be a nice little pussy-cat! I want that most of all. (*dancing around impatiently.*) Open it! Oh, do open it quickly!

The Emperor—Gently! Gently! You nearly trod on my toes just now. (*The men open the casket, showing a rose-tree with one rose in bloom.*)

One Maid of Honor—Oh, what a sweet pink color!

Another—So delicate!

Another—And how prettily it is made!

The Emperor—It is more than pretty, it is charming . . . so poetic!

The Princess (touching the leaves)—O Papa! It isn't made at all: it is a natural flower—a common thing—there are heaps like that in the garden.

The Attendant—May it please your Highness, this rose tree is not like other roses. It was taken from the grave of the Prince's father; it only blossoms once in every five years, and its scent is so sweet that, whoever smells it, forgets all care and sorrow in a moment.

The Princess—I haven't any cares or sorrows, so you can take it away again; I don't want it, and I don't believe its anything but a common garden plant. You can tell the Prince that I won't marry him; and if he come to see me he can go away again, for I won't see him. Now you can go! I am tired of silly presents and princes.

(*Exit Servants with casket.*)

The Emperor—You are a very rude girl!

The Princess (catching him by the hands and making him dance)—No, I'm not. . . . You are only pretending to be cross, you dear old Papa!

The Emperor—Stop! stop! You take my breath away!

The Princess (obeying)—Very well; you see what a good daughter I am! I do exactly what you tell me. There (*pushing him into chair.*) Sit down and I will make you tidy! (*putting his crown straight, and looking at him, head on one side.*) You are really very handsome, you know,

Papa, when you don't look cross. (*To the Maids*) Don't you think so?

The Maids (in chorus)—Yes! Yes! He is really very handsome!

The Princess—There! You see, they all think as I do! (*A knock; enter two other Servants with silver casket.*)

The Emperor—Why! Here's another present for you, my dear. Let us see what this is. It may be something more to your liking.

The Princess—No! No! Wait, if it is another rose I shall send it back at once.

The Servant—Your Highness, this is a nightingale that our Prince has sent you: it sings more beautifully than any other bird in the world.

The Princess—What is it made of?

The Servant—Made of . . . ?

The Princess—Yes, what is it made of, stupid? Gold or silver, or diamonds or what?

The Servant—Your Highness, this is a real nightingale.

The Princess (shrilly)—What! An ugly brown thing with feathers and a beak?

The Servant—It sings most beautifully.

The Princess (angrily)—No, no! Take it away; I won't have it.

The Emperor—Let us hear it once, my love.

The Princess (stamping her foot)—Take it away *at once*. And tell the Prince he needn't send me any more presents like that. A gold bird or a silver one that you can wind up would be much nicer. (*more angrily still.*) What are you staring at? Take it away at once, or I shall *scream*.

The Emperor—My dear child, pray calm yourself! (*To the Servants*) Take it away, I beg of you: the Princess is not very well to-day. (*Exit Servants.*)

The Princess (crossly)—Nonsense, Papa, there is nothing the matter with me. (*another knock.*) Oh! If that is another present from the Prince, it shan't come in. (*Enter Prince disguised as Swineherd. His face is stained with brown and smudged with black. His clothes are ragged and old.*)

The Prince—Good day to you, my lord the Emperor! Can you give me work to do in the palace?

The Emperor (stroking his beard)—Why . . . yes . . . Hum! That is lucky! I want some one to take care of the pigs, for we have a great many of them. Yes, you shall be appointed Imperial Swineherd.

The Prince—Good . . . er . . I mean
. . . thank you, your Majesty; I have been
looking for work for a long time.

The Princess (to the Maids)—That is why
he has such a dirty face, I suppose.

The Maids—And look at his clothes . . .
Ugh!

The Emperor—There is a little hut, close to
the pigsties: you can have that for a house if you
like.

The Prince—Thank you, that will suit me very
well. I want somewhere to work.

The Princess—What do you work at, Swineherd?

The Prince—Sometimes I make things that
pretty princesses like to buy: rattles and toys,
and magic pots and pans, and musical boxes.

The Princess—Well, we shall see: if you make
pretty things I shall certainly buy them, but you
don't look as if you could do anything except
take care of pigs. I hope you wash your hands
before you work.

The Emperor—My love! My love! You are
too forward. Run away now and play; the rain
has stopped, and the garden will be looking
pretty. Swineherd, you may go to your work.

The Prince—Thank you, your Majesty.

(*Exit Left.*)

The Princess (calling after him)—I shall come and see your pretty things to-morrow Swineherd! (*She picks up ball, throws it at the Emperor, hitting him, and runs out Right, laughing, followed by Maids.*)

The Emperor (with a big sigh, rubbing his head)—It is certainly high time she was married!

Curtain.

SCENE—*Outside the Swineherd's Hut.*

(Entrances, *Left* and *Right*. When the curtain rises the Prince is discovered sitting on an old stool in the doorway of the hut. He is polishing a small iron pot or pan.)

The Prince—There's a good day's work for you! (*looking at the pot.*) Aha! my fine, my delicate Princess, you will have to pay for this. I can't sell such valuable goods for nothing. But what proud ways and looks she has! she must be humbled. My castle is not big enough to hold such a grand lady . . . Well, porridge-pot (*holding up pot*), she shall pay a hundred kisses for you, neither more nor less, and then we shall see what we shall see: a good many things can happen to princes in disguise. Dear! (*with a sigh*) it is a pity she is so spoilt: she would make me a fine wife and a pretty one too.

The Princess (off the stage)—Come along! Quickly now, this way! I want to see what the creature has made to-day. (*The Prince starts whistling, and rubbing the pot. Enter Princess followed by Maids of Honor. They stand in a group, watching: the Prince takes no notice, but seems busy whistling and working.*)

The Princess (after a pause)—Swineherd! (*The Prince starts, looks up, and then begins working again.*)

The Princess (more sharply)—Swineherd! Don't you know who is talking to you?

The Maids (in chorus)—He has not any manners!

The Princess (going nearer)—What have you got there?

The Prince—A porridge-pot, your Highness.
(whistles and rubs again.)

The Princess (disappointed)—A porridge-pot! What a stupid thing! Have you not a musical box? (*angrily.*) Stop whistling this moment, and answer me: I can't stand near nasty pigsties for ever.

The Prince—This is all I have made to-day,

Princess, but if you will wait a moment I shall show you what it can do. (*goes into hut, coming back again quickly with a jug of very hot water which he pours into the pot.*)

The Princess—What can a silly old porridge-pot do?

The Prince (placing it on a stool)—You will see, if you come close and put your finger on the edge of it. (*The Princess obeys, holding up her long skirt and stepping daintily.*)

The Princess (with her finger on the pot)—Oh! Delightful! Listen, all of you! The Chamberlain is having cutlets for dinner to-day: the Treasurer, French soup (I always thought he was a stingy thing): the Court Herald, eggs and bacon and radishes and tea. . . .

The Maids (in chorus, clapping hands)—Delightful! Charming! How do you know, dear Princess?

The Princess—The pot tells me. The Tailor is having roast beef and Yorkshire pudding: the Cobbler, ham sandwiches and . . . Oh what a lovely pot!

The Maids (putting their fingers on)—The Emperor will have bread and milk and honey for supper: the Chamberlain . . .

The Princess (interrupting)—Yes, yes, I know. Oh, and listen, the pot is singing now Hush! Ah! this is my piece too; I play it with one finger (*dancing round in time and singing*)

Air—'Duncan Gray.'

Tra la la la la la la . . . .

The Prince—It sings much louder if it is put on the fire.

The Princess—I must have it for my own, that is very certain.

The Maids—Yes, yes!

The Princess—What will you take for it, Swineherd?

The Prince—A hundred kisses from your Highness is my price.

The Princess—That is absurd: you are out of you senses. (*walks away followed by the Maids. The Prince takes up the pot as if to enter the hut with it. He whistles same tune as the pot.*)

The Princess (hearing it and coming back)— I will give you my gold ball for it (*Prince shakes his head*), and my golden casket, and my ring with the rubies.

The Prince—A hundred kisses.

The Princess (as if thinking aloud)—Well, I suppose I must be kind to the poor; I am the Emperor's daughter. (*To the Prince*) I will give you ten kisses, and you may take the rest from the ladies of the Court.

The Maids—No, no, we should not like that at all.

The Princess (sharply)—What are you grumbling at? If I can kiss him, surely you can.

The Prince—A hundred kisses from the Princess or I keep the pot.

The Princess—No, you won't; I must have it. (*To the Maids*) Stand round me, then, and spread out your dresses so that no one may see.

(*They do so. The Prince kneels.*) Now count, and be sure you count rightly.

The Maids—One, two, three, four, etc. (*As the counting goes on, enter the Emperor. They are all too busy to notice him.*)

The Emperor (stopping in surprise)—Whatever is all this noise about? What are they doing near the pigsties? (*goes closer on tiptoe.*)

The Maids—Eighty-two, eighty-three, eighty-four, eighty-five, eighty-six.

The Emperor—What is this? Well I never! (*boxes the Princess's ear with his slipper.*)

The Princess (with a cry)—O Papa!

The Emperor (in a great rage)—Don't call me Papa again: I won't have it. I never heard of such a thing . . . an Emperor's daughter kissing a Swineherd? Off with you both, I shall have nothing more to do with you.

The Princess (beginning to cry)—O Papa! I . . .

The Emperor—Not a word, Miss, not another word. If you are so fond of the Swineherd you shall marry him; I will have nothing more to do with you; you are no daughter of mine. March! March, I say!

The Princess (crying bitterly)—I will never do it again . . . Oh! . . . Oh!

The Emperor (angrier than ever)—Do it again if you like . . . a thousand times . . It doesn't matter to me. You shall not enter my doors again. (*To the Maids*) Come, all of you, and don't huddle there like scared rabbits. Follow me, and if one of you dare speak to that girl again, out you go, neck and crop! (*drives them all before him to Left.*)

The Princess (running after him and catching his gown)—Don't leave me! Oh, don't leave me!

The Emperor (pulling himself away from her)

—If you and your Swineherd are not out of here in half an hour, I shall send soldiers to chase you.

(exit.)

The Princess (crouching on the ground, still crying)—Oh! . . . Oh! . . . What an unhappy girl I am! . . . If I had only married the handsome young prince!

The Prince—Well, it is no use crying, you will have to come with me now. It serves you right: you laughed at the Prince's gifts, and yet you would kiss a common man like me for the sake of a porridge-pot.

The Princess (stopping her sobs)—Why? How do you know that?

The Prince—I know many things. Come, get up: we have a long way to walk before we get home.

The Princess—I am not going home with *you*.

The Prince—You will have to: who else will take you in?

The Princess—I don't care: I will starve, or die; I'll do anything, but I won't marry you.

The Prince—Nobody asked you to: I won't have you for my wife. Come along (*pulling her up*), you shall be my servant and clean my house and cook my dinner.

The Princess (bursting into tears again)—O Papa! Papa! How could you be so cruel!

The Prince—He won't hear you, however loud you cry; you have to come with me. Here, take the pot, I have other things to carry. (*puts it in her hands, enters the hut, and comes out again with package.*)

Now, step out, or the soldiers will chase us. (*takes her hand and pulls her out by Right.*)

Curtain.

Eighty-two, eighty-three, eighty-four, eighty-five, eighty-six.—Page 141

The Surprise

DRAMATIS PERSONÆ

DINAH.
PATIENCE.
EDITH.
JACK.
PEGGY.
DICK.
HAROLD.
LUCY.

THE SURPRISE.*

Enter Dinah, on tiptoe.

Din.—Nobody knows what I know.

Enter Harold.

Din.—Hush, Harold, hush!

Har.—What is it?

Din.—It's a surprise.

Har.—A surprise?

Din.—Yes, we're going to be surprised.

Har.—How do you know?

Din.—Because I saw the cage.

Har.—The cage! what cage?

Din.—The cage the hens are in.

Har.—The hens! which hens?

Din.—The hens mammy is going to give us.

Har.—Is she going to give us some hens?

Din.—Yes! and a cock!

Har. (clapping his hands).—Oh!

Din.—But mind you mustn't say a word about it—it's a great secret——

Har.—Take care! there's Lucy coming.

---

*The characters in this play can be acted either by girls or boys, the names being changed.

147

Enter Lucy.

Din. and Har.—Sh—sh! Sh—sh!

Lucy—What is it? Why are you saying "Sh!"
like that?

Din.—We've got a secret.

Lucy—A secret! what sort of secret?

Har.—A secret in a cage.

Din.—You naughty boy! hold your tongue!

Lucy—In a cage! It's a bird then!

Har.—Take care! here's Edith!

Enter Edith.

Din., Har. and Lucy.—Sh—sh!! Sh—sh!!

Edith—What is it! What's the matter?

Din.—We've got a secret.

Har.—You naughty girl! hold your tongue!

Lucy—They won't tell me what it is. It must
be a bird, because it's in a cage.

Edith—In a cage! It might be a wild beast.

Din. and Har.—A wild beast! ha, ha!

Edith—Well, how should I know what it is, if
you don't tell me?

Lucy—Let's try to guess.

Har. (to Din.)—After all, if they guess right
it won't be our fault.

Din.—No, that's true.

Edith—Is it a bird?

Har.—Of course it's a bird, you stupid!

Edith—I'm not stupid—it might have been a squirrel. Squirrels are in cages sometimes.

Har.—Of course, it *might* have been a crocodile, but it isn't.

Lucy—Is it a canary?

Har.—Bigger.

Edith—A thrush?

Din.—Bigger.

Har.—Take care! there's Peggy .

Enter Peggy.

All—Sh—sh! sh—sh!

Peggy—What is it? What's the matter?

Lucy—We're guessing a secret.

Har.—Trying to guess it, you mean.

Edith—It's something in a cage.

Peggy—Oh, I'll guess too! Is it a pigeon?

Din.—Bigger.

Peggy—What does it do?

Din.—It surprises us.

Peggy—I mean what noise does it make?

Har.—It makes us say Sh—sh!

Edith—Take care! there's Dick coming!

Enter Dick.

All—Sh—sh! sh—sh!

Dick—What is it? what are you doing that for?

Lucy—We've got a secret.

Din.—A secret that we won't tell you.

Dick—Then you're very rude indeed. I don't like rude people.

Ed.—Try and help us to guess it.

Dick—What sort of a thing is it? The last time we had a secret it was some knitted slippers for Pappy. Is this secret a pair of slippers, or a woolen comforter?

Har. Oh, you *are* a stupid child!

Din.—How could a pair of slippers get into a cage?

Dick—Quite easily, if anyone put them there.

Lucy—Well, it isn't a pair of slippers.

Din.—Take care! take care! there's Jack!

Jack comes in mysteriously.

All—Sh—sh! sh—sh!

Jack—What are you making that noise for? Why are you all behaving like steam-engines in a station?

Din.—We've got a secret.

Jack—Have you? So have I.

All—Have you? What is it about?

Jack—Ha! I won't tell you.

Din.—Then we won't tell you ours.

Jack—Is yours a nice secret?

Har.—Lovely!

Din.—It's a surprise mammy's got for us.

Jack—It must be a good big secret if it takes so many of you to keep it.

Lucy—Do tell us yours, Jack!

Edith—There's a good boy!

Jack—Then you must tell me yours afterwards.

Din.—Very well, we will.

Jack—All right, then, come here and I'll tell.

    [*Beckons them all round him mysteriously.*

Jack—You must know that as I went along the back passage I saw a curious-looking parcel.

All—A parcel!

Jack—So I bent down to look. I listened—

All—Listened!

Jack—And peeped.

All—Peeped!

Jack—There was a great flapping and pecking going on inside!

All—Flapping and pecking!

Jack—And then what do you think I heard?

All—What?

Jack—Cock-a-doodle-doo!

Peggy—A cock?

Jack—Yes! a cock and some hens.

Din.—The cock and hens mammy is going to give us!

Dick—Is she going to give us a cock and hens?

Din.—Yes! that was our secret too!

Har.—That's the surprise!

Enter Patience.

Patience—Quick, quick, all of you! Mammy wants you! she's got a great surprise for you!

All—Oh, the cock and hens! How nice!

Patience—Why, do you know what the surprise is already?

Jack—It won't be much of a surprise if we all know what it is.

Din.—What a pity! What shall we do.

[*All reflect.*

Har.—I have it! Instead of mammy surprising us, we'll surprise her, by telling her we know her secret! That will come to just the same thing.

Din.—Oh, what a good idea!

All—Quick! let's go and surprise mammy!

[*Exeunt, running.*

$$\frac{116}{65^{t}} - \text{par copy}$$

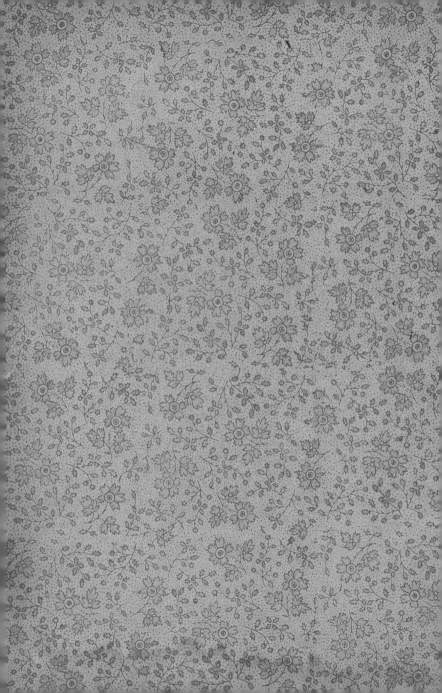